MINDSPLOITATION

Asinine Assignments For The Online Homework Cheating Industry

Published by Seven Footer Press
247 West 30th Street
Second Floor
New York, NY 10001

First printing March 2013
10 9 8 7 6 5 4 3 2 1

© 2013 Vernon Chatman
All rights reserved.

Cover, Layout, and Illustrations by David OReilly

ISBN 978-1-934734-91-9

www.sevenfooterpress.com

MINDSPLOITATION

Asinine Assignments For The Online Homework Cheating Industry

By Vernon Chatman

Introduction

By Louis C.K.

I've known Vernon Chatman for almost a decade. What always amazes me about Vernon is that he will have an idea and then he'll actually do it. This book is a very good example of that.

This book is awesome, it's entertaining (I haven't read this book) and hilarious. Vernon explained to me that this book is about getting online services to write essays for him based on ridiculous premises.

Hold on a second, I need to read at least some of it or this is just dishonest. Hold on please. I mean, I realize that the passage of time between this and the next sentence will not be experienced by you reading it as it is by me writing it — so I don't really need to tell you to wait — because, like a miraculous time machine, you will be able to go from this sentence to the next, though written a whole day apart, in an instant.

See? This is now the next day. I'm writing this a day later than the part right before this. And yet, for you it was no time at all.

The only trouble is that I promised to read some of Vernon's book in the time I was away. But I didn't. I didn't do much of anything. I ate some Tate's chocolate chip cookies. I googled my own name. I took a long nap. Like eight hours. (I guess that was actually me sleeping.) But I didn't read Vernon's book. Okay. I'm sorry. I'll read some of it now. Again, please just... don't do anything. But I'm going to go read the book and then come back.

Hi. I'm back. It's been six months since I wrote that last sentence. A lot has changed in those six months. But again, to you reading this, no time has gone by. Unless you put this down yourself and went away and then came back to it.

Okay. Enough. I have read some, but not all, of Vernon's book. It's really good. See, Vernon is not only a very creative guy, but also a selfless and generous guy.

FDR once said, "There is no end to what you can accomplish if you're willing to give other people the credit." Vernon's book is a creative version of this. Most writers are self-obsessed and they believe their writing comes from some golden spring in their brains. But Vernon is more interested in what creative work he can make come out of other people's brains. He's a comedy sociologist. Do we need a comedy sociologist? Maybe not. But having one, or reading a book by one, will never give AIDS to a baby or make a hurricane ruin a library.

The bottom line is, this book exists. And you are reading it. That is the only fact you can be entirely certain of. As long as your brain is occupied by processing these words, nothing else is even real. So just keep reading and maybe your wife didn't leave you after all. And by the way, stop telling people your wife left you when they say "how are you?" Just say "I'm fine." Don't bum everyone out. Jesus.

Okay. I think the bottom of the page is coming soon. Which means I have to go. I have to go over there. To the part of the room that I am pointing at.

And I'm not taking this computer with me so I won't be writing anymore. Yes, it's a laptop, and I could bring it over there and keep writing. But that's not the point.

The bottom of the page is coming.

See how close I am to it?

My god. It's so awful.

How a page just ends.

It just stops.

My god.

The author would like to thank the following horrible companies for assisting in the creation of this manuscript:

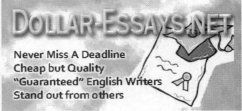

ATTENTION

Dearest Reader,

Years ago when I attended college, my classmates and I never shirked our responsibilities. Every day we rolled up our sleeves and took the initiative to employ only the most thoughtful and diligent online custom-essay-writing companies to do our homework for us - at a hefty price per page. Recently however, social standards have nose-dived butt-first into a dramatic turn for the craven, evidenced by how the *legitimate* online cheating industry has become overrun by cheap, barely-competent, non-native English-speaking netizens of such backwater hick towns as *Bangalore*, *Pakistan*, and *New Jersey*.

As a vital service to mankind, I have taken valuable time out of my busy schedule of throwing cranberries to the ceiling and catching them in my mouth to put these new companies to the test, under a panoply of clever aliases, and at my own expense. The results of this noble outsourcing experiment are presented here wholly unedited. What follows are **100% REAL exchanges with <u>actual online essay writing companies</u>** – *with all errors carefully preserved in the interest of scientifical accuracy*.*

Kindly hold your applause until the end of the book,

VERNON V CHATMAN IV

Contents

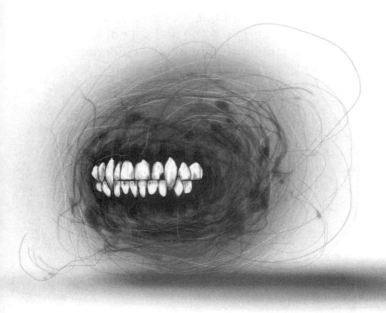

ASSIGNMENT 01: PERSONAL TRAGEDY
Private Reflections On The Death of My Beloved Grandmother

Dear EssayHelpers,

I need you guys to write a essay for my "Personal Journalism In 21st Century Heartsong" class. It's a fairly standard EDPT (Emotionally Devastating Personal Tragedy) essay assignment:

"Movingly explore the deep psychological scars, intense emotional trauma, fruity philosophical insights, and sneaky hidden fees of losing a loved one OR family member to the ravages of Dame Death (the same fate that awaits us all, lurking neath every shadow bah ha ha...)".

Ew, right? I volunteered to write about the death of my beloved grandma Grace Von Chewby, before I realized I am just too dang heartsick to scrape together enough cold-eyed eloquence to earn me more than a C+ (I'm going for an A on this — as a tribute to her gentle face). So I'm calling in you guys to do it.

A few details you gotta know about her for the essay: She was a cruel woman, but short. She always used to tickle her 18 kitties till they collapsed into spastic piles of hysterical laughter. This was how she made her living, somehow. (Maybe thru tips...?) Write about how she could make anyone smile (or breakfast) with just a 5 dollar bill (or some eggs). Legend has it she once killed a duck with just a pack of cards, a peanut, a stopwatch, a blowgun, and a hammer. (It had waddled into her rose garden and greedily eaten a cherry pie she had set out to cool on the edge of her lip.) Also she sheehefhhg shhhii ffkskd hidngdi... (See? I can't write about her! It's too painful!!) You guys do it.

Cook up any other particulars you fancy, just make sure the essay becomes mankind's most profound statement concerning the frightening specter of every child's looming oblivion reflected in the glassy, lifeless eyes of his elders. And try not to use the C-word. If I get a good grade, I may use the essay–with a few tweaks–as a eulogy for my other grandma (Ruth "Da Toof") who, as luck wouldn't have it, is in the next room dying of chili poisoning as I type these hallowed words.

Gracias Mucho Con Carne,
Vincent Chaman

RE: ORDER 20734

Dear Vincent Chaman,

We are pleased to inform you that your order for custom
writing services, for the topic 'Personal Tragedy Essay
For Journalism Class (Private Reflections On The Death of
My Beloved Grandmother)', has been confirmed by EssayHelpers.
You should expecting delivery of the completed Essay by
Friday. You have unlimited free revisions.

EssayHelpers

RE: RE: ORDER 20734

Dear EssayHelpers,

Awesome guys, I look forward to checking it out!   I can't wait to read the essay and find out what emotions my tragic loss has caused in me! In fact, when I told my other grammers (my Bubby Ruth "Da Toof" Chaman) that I was paying YOU to compose this essay she got so worked up that she just... sorta... passed away. So I'm PUMPED that this "one stone" will definitely be the demise of a duo of our fine feathered and be-beaked friends! (Translation – look out "2 old birds", I gots me a rock to kill both of you with!)   I scored a "Toof-er"!!

You're literally saving my life (and by "life" I literally mean "ass") on this!

Grammy® is looking down her nose from heaven on you!

Vincent Chaman

Personal Tragedy Essay

Human relationships are always strong with the near and dear ones. I example, have close affiliation and emotional attachment with my grandmother. I never thought that she would leave me in this way because I always found her quite close to me, rather side by side, everywhere. She remained in my senses.

My grandma died of Alzheimer's disease at 73 where, as the person gets older he forgets all that he left behind, all the cherished traces of life's leftovers are washed away in the back of one's mind. She was very nurturing. My memories of my grand mother include her either cleaning the house in a skirt or cooking also. She always mad people laugh with her senses of humor. She would always yell at me and say she would hit me with wooden spoon. I could talk to her about almost everything.

In its benign days, I thought it was just a normal thing with her as she used to forget my name, thinking that all people behaved that way. Gradually, I realized that this was not the case and my nightmare came true when she was diagnosed with the disease.

I feel lucky to have had the experience of serving my dearest grandmother and to have all of those sweat memories. My holiday will never be the same without her cooking Italian.

The time that follows seeing death can be filled with a stunned belief even if it is not until later that the emotional feelings reveal themselves. Some people need to actually see the body of the deceased in order for the death to register.

The loss of a loved one is an earthquake that fracture our emotional landscape. Although death is the most permanent loss we face, there are other forms of loss that can be devastating as well. The most common for children are moving and divorce. When adults decide to move or separate, after gradually adjusting to the transition, children have no choice but to accept their decision.

RE: RE: ORDER 20734

Hi My Writers,

Great Job!! Killer first draft. How did you know my grandma used to hit me with wooden spoon?! I still pick the splinters out of my deformed cheek to this day. Your essay was so touching to read — it felt like she was there hovering over me. It was as though I could feel her hot grey breath on my neck. Thank God that turned out to just be BigGuy, my pet chipmunk, perched on my shoulder panting into my mouth. Yuck. ...OK, I just fed him a whole bunch of mints... He ain't breathing at all now. I suppose he'll never breathe again. Thats on your hands.

Only a few tiny problems with the essay: My grandma ("Grendle" we called her [mention it]) did not die of Alzheimer's. I don't know where you got that rubbish (everyone knows its not a fatal disorder, just degenerative. Heck, maybe YOU'VE got Alzheimer's - ha! Though if you do, I'm sorry cuz it's no laughing matter). She was in fact killed by being slammed into by a speeding bus. (She would've survived, but it hit her right in the body.) I do believe the elderly, disoriented bus driver suffered both Alzheimer's and eczema. (So I guess, in a way, she DID die from Alzheimer's — indirectly! HA!)

Anyhoo, could you re-do it? Put in the part about her getting creamed by the bus as it headed towards Disneyland. The irony is, even before the "accident" Grandma Grendle resembled a shoe full of cream. In even better news, my mom gave me the go-ahead to use this essay as my OTHER grandma's eulogy — but I'll need this new rewritten draft ASAFP. (Services are Sunday, and I'm not gonna even peek at your new draft until I'm up at the podium during the funeral, reading it aloud, so it feels natural — and so I'm not bored). Can't wait to read it — this is gonna be DOPE, yo!!

Sincerely (PSYCHED),

Vincent Chaman

P.S. I can tell your parents are divorced.

RE: RE: RE: ORDER 20734

Dear Vincent Chaman,
We have successily gone through the changes suggested by you.
Attached is your updated paper. We hope that you've enjoyed
our service. We will be looking forward to see you once again.

EssayHelpers

Personal Tragedy Essay 2

Human relationships are always strong with the near and dear ones. I example, have close affiliation and emotional attachment with my grandmother. We used to call her "Grandma Grendle". I never thought that she would leave me in this way accidentally because I always found her quite loving me.

My grandma died in a bus accident at 73 where, as the person gets oldert he forgets all that he left behind, all the cherished traces of life's leftovers are washed away in the back of one's mind. The bus was headed towards Disneyland. She was very nurturing. My memories of my grand mother include her either cleaning the house in a skirt or cooking also. She resembled cream in a shoe. She always mad people laugh with her senses of humor. She would always yell at me and say she would hit me with wooden spoon. I could talk to her about almost everything.

In its benign days, I thought it was just a normal thing with her as she used to forget my name, thinking that all people behaved that way. Gradually, I realized that this was not the case and my nightmare came true when she died in a bus accident.

I feel lucky to have had the experience of serving my dearest grandmother and to have all of those sweat memories. My holiday will never be the same without her cooking Italian.

The time that follows seeing death can be filled with a stunned belief even if it is not until later that the emotional feelings reveal themselves. Some people need to actually see the body of the deceased in order for the death to register.

The loss of a loved one is an earthquake that fracture our emotional landscape. Although death is the most permanent loss we face, there are other forms of loss that can be devastating as well. The most common for children are moving and divorce. When adults decide to move or separate, after gradually adjusting to the transition, children have no choice but to accept their decision.

RE: RE: RE: RE: RE: ORDER 20734 (revised)

Hey guys,

So, the funeral service was the most balls-out tasteful affair I ever saw!! Not that it was a competition — but I pretty much won the whole ceremony when I stood up and read my essay (wink - YOUR essay), which everyone thought was so moving that some people actually started moving out of the room — probably to go buy tissues from the tissue stand I set up in the lobby ($$$$!).

I took the liberty of covering the back of my neck with scotch tape this time before I read the essay, so I wouldn't have that creepy "dead-Grandma's-breath-on-my-neck" sensation again. I should have done it before I got up on the podium to speak, but everyone just watched with their jaws respectfully hung open as I did it.

Once I started reading, I killed! I hope you don't mind, but I added a smidge to your words on the fly — threw in a couple dozen limericks to break the ice. And I couldn't resist whipping BigGuy out of my slacks' pocket to do a couple tricks — the "*shimmy*", the "*mashed potato*", the "*primal scream*", etc... He's sure starting to rot!

Later, at the reception (free shrimp!) one old guy even glared at me like he wanted my autograph, but he was so nervous to ask that he dozed off in his wheelchair as I was telling him a little bit about myself. So I just silently signed his breasts and pushed him away, to preserve my mystique.

But listen: Your essay was so emotional that I am worried about whether you were gonna be OK, or if you needed to rap about your feelings? I can tell that divorce hit you pretty hard... so, just... KNOW that I am always here for you, OK? For rapping? I have no one else in my life, so it's really no trouble. Please reach out to me. Please. You're all I've got.

ASSIGNMENT 02: BIOENGINEERING BASICS

Crossbreeding 101

Hey HomeworkRelievers,

So I am taking this Bioengineering class. And I kind of told my professor that I have been spending the last few months at home trying to breed a mouse with a chameleon lizard. And I've sort of been making all these excuses about why I haven't been showing up to class and doing any of the assignments everyone else in the class has been doing. See, I've been telling him the progress has gone well and that I sprayed the mouse with lizard musk, and last week I told him that the mouse was very pregnant from lizard jism. Anyway, the point is my professor is such a jerk that he doesn't believe me at all.

Well, I have a secret for your eyes only: Not only do I NOT have a pet mouse OR a pet lizard, but my left LEG is NOT prosthetic (as I've been telling him and others for months) nor is it "filled with Skittles".

The ONLY way my professor is going to pass me is if I write a kick butt paper about the results of my (made up) breeding experiment. I, of course, know nothing about bioengineering, so I can't do it. So you have to write a really convincing paper that explains specifically how I bred the two species, and how the mouse got pregnant (describe how they did the act out of true love, NO LURID SMUT) and how the mouse gave birth to these little lizard babies (say what they look like — make it believable, guys) and how she nursed them with her big sweet honking teats, and then one day the mouse and the lizard got in a mega fight and they killed each other so I can't bring them into class as proof because also they ran away from home. Maybe include something about how each baby had an expandable pouch under its chin for carrying chimichangas (the primary source of nutrition for this revolutionary new species).

Me and my big stupid mouth got me in this mess and now you guys gotta climb in there and yank me out. You'll be saving my skin, and not in the way that I save my skin when I get a sunburn and then peel my back and use the big skin sheets to press flowers between, but in the sense that you will be saving me from having to get a prosthetic degree.

Vinnie Champing

Bioengineering Basics

   Instead of attending class, I have been spending
the last few months at my home, where I was trying to
breed a mouse with a chameleon lizard. In these days,
I learned a lot from this experience. Generally, mouse,
name applied to numerous species of small rodents, often
having soft gray or brown fur, long hairless tails, and
large ear. And my mouse was had also same qualities. I
sprayed the mouse with lizard musk. After few days the
mouse became pregnant. This experience helped me to ob-
serve this process very closely. My mouse is extensively
used in biological and medical experimentation and I
also kept as pet.

   My breeding experiment became significant due to love
and hate among my pet mouse and chameleon lizard. Chameleons have laterally flattened bodies and bulging,
independently rotating eyes. They are ornamented with
crests, horns, and spines. Chameleons are unique among
lizards in possessing very long, sticky tongues with
which they capture their prey.

   I bred these two species. Chameleon lizard most of
the times attracted my mouse and kissed her many times.
Slowly and gradually their love converted into the process of mating, and the mouse gave birth to many little
lizard babies. These babies were so beautiful at the
time of birth. Their eyes and colors were different. One
day, I saw that she nursed them with her teats. And, I
really became so much impressed. But, unfortunately my
mouse and the lizard started fighting over a chew toy
and they killed each other and all the babies died also.
Therefore, I can't bring them into the class. They are
gone forever.

ASSIGNMENT 03: LITERATURE O'DENSITY
Power Of The Word

Dear EssayExcellence,

I am taking a class called *"Communicative Concision As It Relates To The Literature Of Brevity That Is Concerning The Power Of Succinct Density In Prose And Whatnot (An Applied Appreciation Of Idiomatic Compactness In The Field Of The Written Word, Terseness In Authorship, Getting Quickly To The Epistolary Point, Tightness In Compositional Minimalism As Opposed To Verbose Long Windedness, OR Soul Of Wit Which Is Short In The Tooth)"*. Its hard. And so what I'm gonna need you all to go ahead and do is that I'm going to I need you guys to go ahead and do this one particular assignment that is too hard for me to do, which is why I need you to go on and go ahead and do it for me, instead of me doing it.

The assignment is that we have to read everything that has ever been written about love, and then we are supposed to have a meaningful series of passionate affairs, and then write a paper that sums up all that mankind knows about the topic of love in ONE WORD.

Our teacher is basing 98.7% of our grade on this assignment, and I am completely blocked. I sit in front of my typewriter, but the word just doesn't flow out of me. On the contrary, whiskey flows into me. Every letter on my keypad laughs at me. I glare back at the snickering keyboard, and I'm all like, "What?!! Do I have a joke written on my forehead?" (The answer is no. It's just a funny birthmark.)

The word must be in ALL CAPS in the center of the otherwise blank page. The word must thwack the reader in the nards of the heart like a swinging sack of oranges, causing the reader to stumble face first into the dirt (without leaving any incriminating bruises — no cops on this one). It must literally take the reader on a blistering roller coaster ride across space and time, changing mankind forever. Also, make sure it is spelled correctly. And you CANNOT use the letter "L". And please — I shouldn't have to say this — but: keep it clean.

Vatman Chernis

SURVIVAL

RE: Assignment-119565

Halfhearted Salutation [concealing deep disappointment],

I was very, very, very, very excited to receive the assignment on "Lit O' Den" (LoD), which I had confidently fobbed off onto your capable, if amoral, hands. But it seems, I fear, that you lot are the ones who have proven to be dense — in the mindbrains! Once I got your delivery of my assignment, I printed it up and I set the paper on my bedside with the intent to read it before I dropped off for my nightly sleepy go bye-bye.

I am normally a slow reader, but I launched enthusiastically into reading your word. I enjoyed the beginning of it, as it kicked off briskly and braced the reader with a searing terseness, effortless wit, and muscular momentum. It was really resonating with me - I found it emotionally moving without slipping into sentimentality, if that makes sense? But once I got about half way through the word, I started to get drowsy and nodded off, before the very end. (I'd had a heroic but exhausting day, literally stamping out testicular cancer in my landlord.)

When I awoke a few days later and got around to reading the rest of the word, I was horrified to discover that as a grisly twist ending YOU BROKE THE ONE RULE of the assignment and used the letter "L". I told you this was *verboten*, but I guess that was all French to you. When I first saw that ugly "L" sitting on the page like a turd on a wedding cake, I couldn't believe my EYES — those filthy round scumbags! I stood in the mirror mercilessly accusing my eyes of playing weird mind games on me. I was hard on them, and my hour-long harangue left them flooded with a tide of moisture that would make a 500-gallon backed-up toilet cream its jeans green with jealousy.

Well, I had the paper authenticated and it turns out, mine eyes was right. You guys blew it (and me), plain and simple, hard and fast. Make no miss-take, the first 7/8ths of the word are brilliant - startlingly original, with flashes of genius. But that closing consonant is the worst sort of insult to human decency! I consider it a personal slap to my face, the faces of my parents (who have fragile face bones), and the faces of my unborn children (two of which have yet to even be conceived, you sickos). Please do it again.

Vatman Chernis

RE: RE: Assignment-119565a

Dear Vatman,

We have successfully gone through the changes suggested by
you. Attached is your updated paper. We hope that you've
enjoyed our service. We will be looking forward to see you
once again.

EssayExcellence

DEVOTION

ASSIGNMENT 04: ADBAS
Slogans For New Products

Dear SuperiorSchoolSupport,

In my AdBas (Advertising Basics) class we must create grever (great/ clever) and snatchy (snappy/catchy) slogans for some new, exciting products. Each slogan must grabrod (explain the product) and chewit (use charm, enthusiasm and wit). Here are the products

1. "Brogurt" – this product is a pitch-black yogurt specially designed for black people to eat.

2. "BabbooHeartHam" This is simple: Just some ham in the shape of baboon hearts.

3. "The Ouija Squeegee" – a device that allows the restless dead to clean your car windshield by scrawling messages from the afterworld about their "unfinished business" into the accumulated filth.

4. "16 Foot Party Nugget" – a chicken nugget long enough to satisfy hundreds simultaneously.

5. "Remote Controlled Baby Stroller" – a stroller that makes it so you don't have to be anywhere near your child while you take it out for a frolic.

6. "Speed Lifing" – this is a speed dating service where after your Speed Date, you Speed Marry and Speed Have Kids and Speed Grow Old Together and Speed Pass Away surrounded by loved ones. And the best part is you get all of this in before lunch.

Vishad Chieftan

Advertising Slogans For Innovative Product

Brogurt — "Creamy midnight packed in a tub. Finally, yogurt for the black!"

BabbooHeartHam — "When you want ham to be not ham... let the Baboons roam wild... while you enjoy their hearts between your sandwich!"

The Ouija Squeegee — "Let the arms of the dead work for you with the super and natural power to clean your windscreen!"

16 Foot Party Nugget: — "The nugget so fulfilling, your guests will need a passport to eating it!"

Remote Controlled Baby Stroller — "Forgot to walk the child when you have better things to do? Have it automatically, it is now possible!"

Speed Lifing — "Why take your time with life on marriage and death when we can get you there quickly when you have better things to do?"

ASSIGNMENT 05: SPECIOUS SPECULATIONS IN WORLD LIT

Dear ClassAdvantage,

Due to certain circumstances beyond my control, I simply don't feel like doing my homework. So, like my dad used to say, (before the wizard's curse, when he still had use of his lip) "YOU do it for me, sister!"

OK, so the assignment I need you to get cracking on is:

Write an essay that details in detail: How Would The Holy Bible Be Different If It Starred The Giant Spider From Kafka's The Metamorphasis Instead Of Jesus As The Lead Character?

In the paper you have to say all the ways in which Jesus's' birth, life, massage, face, taint, and lasting historical impact would be different if he was actually that Giant Spider that's the Star of The Metamorphasis by France Kafka.

Like… would people worship The Metamorphasis like it was The Bible? And then… would that make France like God Almighty because he wrote the Bible? Yuck, you guys - a French God? *Que estupido!*

Would people be healed from blindness if a giant Holy French spider laid one of his 8 hands on their head? Then the first thing they'd see after a life of blindness is a huge assed spider foot? No thanks. I'll stay blind.

In conclusion, I really need a A on this because my parents are threatening to stop sending care packages if my GPA dips below my hat size, in which case I'd have to start buying my own cookies. (That CANNOT happen!!!!!!!!!)

Vender Chenda

Jesus vs. Spider

This interesting paper on Speculations in World Literature requires me to ruminate on how the Bible would be
different if it starred the Big Giant Spider from Franz
Kafka's Metamorphosis instead of Jesus. (Kafka, 1996)

The Metamorphosis is a story about alienation, identi-
ty, and self-imprisonmence. The story of Jesus in the New
Testament bible is also the same. Jesus may have felt im-
prisoned in our world compared to the world he came from,
the Heavenly Kingdom. His taking the shape of a man is
also a kind of metamorphosis, as he converts from God to
Man, much like the roach. This can be compared to Gregor
Samsa's awakening one morning to find himself changed. As
Jesus grow up in the world and had to reconcile with ha-
tred and ridicule, he himself might of changed.
    Gregor's profession as traveling salesman is com-
parable to Jesus' life in mission as he traveled the coun-
tryside preaching the Word of God. The eight legs of the
spider could be compared to the Twelve Apostles who were
Jesus' eyes and ears. The weight on Gregor's life in being the financial head of household is similar to Jesus'
weight impending trial and death. Gregor's working to pay
off his debt is similar to Jesus' mission to pay 'the debt
of the sins of mankind' How Jesus felt as he is condemned
to death is similar to Gregor's alienation by his family.
The public carried on after Jesus' death as if nothing had
happened, much as Gregor's family carried on. In this way
we see they are interchangable.

Works Cited
Kafka, Franz (1996). The Metamorphosis and Other Stories, trans. Donna Freed. New York: Barnes & Noble.
    The New Testament Bible. Gideon Series.

RE: ORDER #39351a1

Dear The Good People Who Write My Essays For Me,

I took in your / my Comparative Lit paper with all the relish I could mustard (I've been eating only condiments since I discovered the disgusting stuff they put in tofu dogs: like the ass and the lips of the soybean.). Reading your interesting essay really hit me in a way I didn't expectorate – I was struck like a fist through a baby's face that <u>Jesus Chris is Lord!</u> I never was a religious person, BUT I always liked spiders and the other creepy crawlies of our world. Mostly cuz (1.) They DON'T judge you, and (2.) They can NOT laugh at you behind your back. You explained Jesus in a way that allowed Him to crawl right into my heart and lay thousands of His tiny slick eggs in there. When they hatched, the babies scampered into every cell of my body and now <u>I Am Going To Heavens!!!</u> Jesus Chris is in my heart and it is GOOD! You (like Kafka) metamorphosed me (like Greg Samosa) into a practicing Christian (insect)! Of course, my mom is pissed that I turned my back on our Jewdaic faith, but I told her she better save that piss and use that piss to piss out the flames of Hell where she is going if she don't smarten up.

Within just a few days of attending church I was voted "Most Christian" by my parish in a <u>landslide election</u> — which I conceived, orchestrated and WON! If there is still any doubt up your brains how Christian I am, read this: *"ohn monhg tup oogngjf jfeiwoaababaa uuunfuiuu emeienein biiiiiibbiiiiiii!"* That's write!! I know how to Type In Tongues!!!

I was so psyched on how you spurted gospel up into me, that I brought a box of 100 spiders into church, and let Them go in the second row. The reaction was not very Christ OR Spider like, I assure you. But I am growing a mustache so I'll soon be able to sneak back into church for Sunday sermons under a *nom de plum*. Yum!

Anyhoo... thanks a wad for saving my soul — I OWE YOU LUNCH,

Vender Chenda

P.S. One fear: after mating, spiders bite the heads off their lovers — so... can I trust the Crucifix hanging over my bed? I eagerly await your theological expertise.

P.P.S. Man... if Jesus had 8 arms, they'd have to use a helluva lotto nails to crucifix him! (almost not worth it, from a financial standpoint.)

ASSIGNMENT 06: CONTROLLED FEAR IN HORROR WRITING

Hey You,

I am currently attending "Harverd University Technical Acadamny And Cosmetic Improv Traffic School". I am a "Woodshoppy" major with a minor in "Particularly Controlled Fear In Horror Fiction Writing". My thesis is due and you "du"des are going to "do" it "4" me. Here's the proposal that I (you) must fulfill in order for me to graduate and prevent the violent wrath of my murderous father and avoid becoming another Statistic('s major).

"Write one sentence that is profoundly viscerally frightening, but only scary enough to raise precisely <u>One Goosebump</u> on the reader, preferably on the small of his back but nowhere near the crack of the large of her arse."

The sentence must raise the goose bump within ten seconds of my instructor reading the sentence, and it must be tall enough that my instructor is able to clip off the goose bump, place it in a teeny little cute roasting pan, broast it to a golden "hue" and feed it to her pet pocket lobster.

Godspeed, you mongrels.

Varden Chemastiano

HORROR INDUCING SENTENCE

When I was a child, my mother used to tell me that ghosts do not exist and I believed her easily, as she was my mother.

RE: Controlled Fear Assignment

Dear Sir or Madame –

I'm writing you from Bloodstone Presbyterian Trauma Hospital And Beefsteak Tomato Outlet. My professor read your sentence. It was waaay overboard. You made it way, WAY too scary…

As her characteristically jaded eyes scanned the demonic words you've inflicted onto that poor page, her very Being was seared by a sharp scalding gale of sheer terror. An ear-slaughtering shriek tore bloodily from her throat the entire time as she plodded to the elevator, rode up 12 floors, got out and flung herself from the window. She would have died on impact, but she was spared - buffeted by a protective layer of _thousands of goosebumps_. Her skin was swimming and roiling with golf ball sized knots of undulating flesh lumps. I think I saw an entire goose emerge honking and dazed from the hide of her shoulder.

The goose ran loose, wild and spastic at first, charged with the bright hyper blush of fresh release from it's cruel cage of nonexistence. Eventually, like all things, it slowed. And loping, it found its groove. It began swaying in a groinular fashion, to some sickeningly sensual Internal Beat: an eternally primal throb to which it sweatingly slaved, gyration by lascivious gyration. We live in a society that has rules concerning decency, good sirs, yet this lewd goose you've unleashed still radiates a yearning steam of smut that approaches such Lambadaic levels that even I was forced to bear a massive gander, resulting in a most unwelcome chubby in my trousers. Now I'm very confused about WHO I AM. This was not part of the assignment.

I fear I am now doomed to Hell.

Thanks a million, guys.

Varden Chemastiano

ASSIGNMENT 07: SOCIO-BODULAR MOVEMENT
Teaching Via Dance Craze

Dear EssayAidExperts,

I am taking a Modern Jazz Dance Theory And Development class. We have learned about the profound sociological impact of dance sensations throughout history. Did you know that during cave times, the "wheel" was a form of "boogie-woogie" before it was a "round rolly thing"? Did you know that the Franco-Prussian war was fought in *5-4 time*? Did you know that the Renaissance was really nothing more than a "weekend hoedown"?

Yes, *Dame Dance* is society's Great Educator. And besides, the kids today don't want to listen to that cold frumpy Frau Reason — they wanna bust a move! But with great woogie comes great responsibility. This is where the phrase "woogsponsibility" comes from. So we need to invent a new dance craze that instructs as well as it funks.
 Our assignment is to <u>invent</u> a dance sensation that will sweep the nation AND teach the young people about: *the impotence of refraining from sexual innercourse.*

1. Give it a name. (I'd like you to call it "The Abstinence Slurp")
2. Describe the motions the body must make to be doing the dance. (Make it sexy)
3. Reveal how the sexy movements of the dance will cause the hot teens who are dancing it to get "turned on" by somber abstinence.
4. Strategize a way in which the dance craze can sweep the nation, or at least spread like the clap.

I would do this assignment myself, but I just broke my leg as I was typing this made-up excuse.

Vander Chalman

New Dance Sensation

Recently has appeared in world new dance sensation that slowly involves more and more people from different countries. It is new frank and anxiously-thrilling dance that help people to open heart, to forget all problems, to feel your body from top to toe. This dance becomes a name — "Tsunami". It is a dance of feelings and passion, the most unpredictable desires and fantasies, and liberation from bad energy.

As to body motions in tsunami- they can be slow, fast, abrupt, but above all emancipated and plastic. Your body must be soft like plasticine and move like a wave. Gradually this wave must pass through all your body from head to legs both across and down. With help of such motions you can acquire a muscular shape and learn this dance without severe, exhausting, unnatural training. When you start to do these motions you will convince that your body looks very attractive.

With this dance you will freed yourself from cumulative energy and bad emotions, because it establish contact with your body and this way you will be free from necessity of constant sexual intercourses.

To sweep the nation in this crazy tsunami dance, dancers must spread the information about this new sensational technique of body independent among young people. They by-turn must involve their friends to this tsunami trend. Also concerned with this technique choreographs must open tsunami clubs with advertisement above the main entrance "Everyone is welcome!" Thereby the wave of popularity of this dance will quickly pass around the world and lead young people not only to dance emancipation, but also to refraining from different intercourses that nowadays very popular among "hot teens".

RE: COMPOSE AD TO SELL RESULT OF DANCE

Dear Dears,

The dance didn't work at all. In fact, it stirred up a tsunami of erotic sauce that sloshed across town resulting in at least 8 pregnancies so far. The bop cops are saying that the babies are my woogsponsibility since I popularized the dance. I don't know how to raise babies, dog! The only thing I know how to make is love, money and water. So I'm going to sell them on craigslist, but I need help writing the ad. Here are the particulars: Make sure the listing mentions they are "slightly used infants" (I don't want people expecting fresh product). Say they're in "good to fair" condition although a few have "slight spine damage" and others are "dog eared". Come up with a good price point per unit, and a bulk discount if someone takes them all off my hands.

The babies have all their papers, but they are not potty trained, so the papers are a mess. They are smog tested and they come in all 4 colors, but can be painted easily.

Make up a bunch more details so irresistible it could make some dude who don't even *like* kids AT ALL say 'what the heck' and drop dime on an impulse buy. I'm going CRAZY! Everything MUST GO! You'd be slurprised, butt lactating hurts, and the poor critters gotta suckle so hard, its not even milk that's coming out — it's got more of a *chili* consistency.

Vander Chalman

Re:RE: COMPOSE AD TO SELL RESULT OF DANCE

hello

sorry, it is not clear from you email, are you going to
sell dog puppies? How many puppies you have total?

Angela Lowrey.
Customer Services

RE:Re:RE: COMPOSE AD TO SELL RESULT OF DANCE

Dear Angela,

Goodness me!! I would _never_ sell puppies online, as if they are meat. If you want to sell meat, do it in a butcher shop, right?

Vander Chalman

P.S. yum!!

Re:RE:Re:RE: COMPOSE AD TO SELL RESULT OF DANCE

sorry, but I do not understand you... so, you want to sell
8 HUMAN babies???

Angela Lowrey.
Customer Services

RE:Re:RE:Re:RE: COMPOSE AD TO SELL RESULT OF DANCE

yo,

babies dog

Vander Chalman

Re:RE:Re:RE:Re:RE: COMPOSE AD TO SELL RESULT OF DANCE

it is the third time Im trying to get an answer: do you
want to sell 8 HUMAN babies???

sorry, but I want to get exact answer from you!!! do
you want to sell HUMAN babies???

Angela Lowrey.
Customer Services

RE:Re:RE:Re:RE:Re:RE: COMPOSE AD TO SELL RESULT OF DANCE

Angela,

I have been as careful as I can to answer your question, and I would like to say as clear as possible: You keep asking me if you can buy human babies from me, and it makes me uncomfortable.

Miss, I don't think that you should be allowed to buy human babies and I don't know why you would want to buy them, since you can make them for free, as a lady. I don't mean to sound angry, but I want you to know that I am furious. There is no good reason whatsoever to try to purchase human babies or to put them on sale, even as meat. Unless you are doing it for a VERY good reason, like if you just need to get rid of them. For example.

But listen: I am not angry at you, although I am. If you are serious about your idea of trying to buy human babies, I would appreciate it if you would stop asking me and go ask someone else, because I wouldn't sell you a human baby even if I *was* selling them, because I don't think you are a good fit for my product. So lets get off the topic of you trying to buy babies and back to the assignment at hand: I just need this ad written for me... for... a school assignment, or something like that.

Vander Chalman

Re:RE:Re:RE:Re:RE:Re:RE: COMPOSE AD TO SELL RESULT OF DANCE

are you kidding me?? in your first messages you wrote
something about selling babies, YOU, not ME!!!! that
is why I asked you few times what its going on! and what
do you want from us? what assignment we should complete?
write an advertisement to sell BABIES!!!!???? or what??

Angela Lowrey.
Customer Services

P.S. It sounds like you are crazy person! I'm going to
inform about you authorities!

RE:Re:RE:Re:RE:Re:RE:Re:RE: COMPOSE AD TO SELL RESULT OF DANCE

Oh *Angela!*

Now I get it! You are doing the *dance*, you wriggling flirt — the familiar push and pull of passion's pirouette, whipping up the winds of precoital consume' into a conjugal tornado. That blasted Tsunami has you in its amorous grip. You do not want to buy a baby — you want to make one, *au naturel*, with yours truly. Well, I say let us give it time - I hardly know you, and this is all moving so fast. I think we should let this relationship blossom organically. And if a child results, so be it. That said, I'm not going to deny that I have feelings for you too, its just that… I have had this happen many times with essay companies before and I've been burned in the past. So inform about me all you like, because my only authority is the human heart. It is not for sale, but I am ready to obey the fluttering letter of its every throbbing law.

Loving you is easy cuz you're Angela Lowery,

Vander Chalman

ASSIGNMENT 08: MED COMMUNICATION TECHNIQUE

Death Informage

Dear Kind Whomever,

I am in medical school. When I intern at the trauma center, one of the main jobs they stick me with is telling people their loved one has died. Yikes, right? In the ER we call this "pulling the ass duty". The hospital admin insists when we break the bad news that we keep it light and jovial, cuz it ain't good for business to have a bunch of weeping crying people flopping around all over the place. The other customers (we are supposed to call them "patients") would turn right around and find another place to treat their medical disasters if they saw a buncha slobbering freaks flipping out in our Luxury Trauma Lounge. So my assignment is to prepare a variety of new, better ways to tell these "loved ones" that the patient *"didn't make it"* or *"passed into deadness"*, AND that also puts a smile on their shattered faces AND shoves a giggle into their devastated hearts.

Please come up with a few fun (and FUNNY) ways to notify folks that their loved one straight up died to death.

Thanks!!

Vinnie Chemin

Medical Communication Techniques

In Medical hospitals today, people receiving sad news about their loved ones being dead, they feel depressed and sometimes lost consciousness about it. The first time they got the news, they only react to the way the doctors bring out the news to them. For example, if a doctor comes out of the ward room, and tells the family of the patient that the patient is dead in a way that he himself feels so sad or scared, the family will feel shock and will lead to losing consciousness and even some of them can become insane for a while. But if the doctor comes out and make the family of the deceased relaxed by telling him/her that the patient passed away explaining that they have to take heart, this news and information from the doctors will make the family of the patient relaxed and won't make anything bad happen at that moment: although they will feel so depressed about the news but it will not make them do anything strange or bad to themselves. That is why it is good to have communications between the doctors and the patients.

Medical doctors are trained to become doctors. If unfortunately the patient dies, they can say in a cool way that they tried to bring him back but he is gone, or he passed away in a cool and gentle way by expressing their sympathy not by telling them officially.

In conclusion, there are different ways to communicate to patient or make them feel alright and these ways will make the people feel happy and it will not affect them mentally.

RE: assignment num.56824

Hey Guys!!

I liked your essay so much I loosed consciousness!!!   I couldn't wait to use your advice, so when I came to, I ran full speed to a medical hospital and found a family who needed to have the news broken to them that their dad was all dead. I whipped out your paper and read it to them. They lost consciousness, so I had to wake them up and read it to them a few more times until they got through hearing the whole thing without losing consciousness. I'm not sure whether they were losing consciousness out of boredom or out of emotional devastation (probably a lil' smidge of each). Then they went insane for a little while. Worst of all, they didn't laugh once. Not cool.

Teacher tells me this was a mistake. The assignment is not complete. You must PROVIDE SPECIFICS of what to say to the victim's families.

You need to please provide several ACTUAL EXACT SENTENCES OF WHAT TO SAY TO VICTIM'S FAMILIES (word for word) to tell them that their loved one has died. Keep it light and VERY FUNNY.

The Hospital staff has provided an example:
"Hey dude, you have a stain on your shirt [then when the gentleman looks down and sees there is no stain, put your arm on his shoulder tenderly and whisper] just kidding — but your son has passed into deadness"

Please hurry because I have a family out in the waiting room who need some really traumatic news broken to them, and I'm just gonna to stall and vamp until I receive your wonderful response. Luckily, I'm really good at doing funny little dances, and back flips, and cracking walnuts on my forehead. But these fun distractions may get old soon, as they await word of their (very dead) loved one.

Vinnie Chemin

Medical Communication Techniques

Like for example, if a man named John was dead and you want to tell his family that John passed away, you can let them know in this way: "Hello. John was a real great man and he really loves women, I feel like he should be here right now to flirt with my nurses like he always does, but I have to say he is gone to greater glory now I am sorry". And in another case if John is not known by the doctor, the doctor can say that, "It is a pleasure to meet a very beautiful woman like you being John's wife and you have this nice kids here who looks so much as handsome as John himself, He is a great man and I regret to tell you this that he has just passed away." Also the doctor can say it in a way that makes it more funny to believe, he just have to smile when he comes out of the room and saying: "I must admit you have a very nice and wonderful day, you all look so beautiful and I bet just the way John looks as well, but I must tell you this that it is good not being so fat like him, anyway he passed away some minutes ago. I am so sorry."

In conclusion, there are different ways to communicate to patient or make them feel alright and these ways will make the people feel happy and it will not affect them mentally.

ASSIGNMENT 09: HUMAN BIOLOGICAL TECHNOLOGISM
Invent A New Limb

Dear PaperAiders,

Each student in my class has to invent a different new limb, in order to bioengineer a more superior human form. I was assigned the task of designing a "new limb with a sole purpose" (like, say, to crack open peanuts). It should be located somewhere below the waist.

In your delightful essay, please answer the following:

- *What does the new limb look like?*
- *What's its name?*
- *What is its purpose?*
- *Where is it located and why?*
- *I'm sorry, I didn't catch that: Why?*
- *Take me through a day in the life of the new limb, won't you?*
- *I'm terribly sorry, my hearing is rather shoddy, can you repeat that?*
- *Any exciting financial possibilities created by the existence of the new limb? Eh, my boy?*

Vibon Childon

INVENT A NEW LIMB

The new limb looks like a claw, which has little blunt claws to crack open peanuts and seeds. The limb is light and it is not sharp. The length of the limb is about two feet depending on the height of the individual. The higher is the individual the longer is the claw.

The name of the limb is the peanutclaw

The purpose of the peanutclaw is to crack open peanuts and seeds. The peanutclaw may be used to hold objects of the small and middle size.

The peanutclaw is located below the waist to take peanuts and seeds easily, crack them open and move them to the mouth of the individual.

The peanutclaw is the universal cracker of peanuts and seeds and holder for objects of the small and middle size.

The day starts with cleaning the peanutclaw. The peanutclaw can be used in the course of the day to hold various objects and to crack open peanuts and seeds. It can be used during the meal.

The financial possibilities of the new limb are diverse. In fact, the new climb may be used as a universal cracker and holder. In addition, it can be used as attraction for those who do not have such a limb.

RE: Invent a New Limb

Gentlemens,

Thank you greatly for your fine work developing the peanutclaw©. It is masterful in concept and elegant in design. I had my peanutclaw© installed this morning, and it has changed my life immeasurably. My peanutclaw© moves with the grace of a gazelle gliding gently through the colon of a swan. Although I have only had my peanutclaw© for 12 hours, I have already eaten my weight in nuts and seeds!

However… One small problem has arisen from the heavenly horizon of this perfection, like a peeved Kraken: My peanutclaw© seems to have a mind of its own. I awoke from my hourly nap today to find my peanutclaw© rooting around in the most intimate nethers of my crotch, presumably on a desperate quest for nuts and seeds to crack and feed its master (me). I became so disturbed and frightened by this, that I immediately needed another nap.

I re-awoke an hour later, shocked to discover that I was being dragged by my (disconcertingly muscular) peanutclaw© across town towards the grocery store, where my peanutclaw© dove claw first into a barrel of irresistible pistachios in a vain attempt to slake its seemingly unquenchable urge for cracking all things *seed and nut*. A base lust for nuts and seeds has driven my peanutclaw© quite insane. This is a peanutclaw© designflaw™. Please write a paper to clarify the powers and intensions of the peanutclaw©, and answer these questions three:

1. Who rules the peanutclaw©?
2. What is the peanutclaw's© prime directive?
3. Is there an off switch on a peanutclaw©? (please… I hope there is)
4. What does peanutclaw© meat taste like?

I hope my peanutclaw© doesn't discover that I am writing about it right now. My peanutclaw© looks like it has a ruthless temper. I fear that the rest of my body is becoming a vestigial appendage, a meek slave to the nut-centric whims of my new Master. It sucks.

If this problem isn't solved technologismistically© I will be forced to hunt the limb down like an animal, extinguish its life, clean the organs from its carcass, cook it, eat it, and wear its hide for treasure.

INVENT A NEW LIMB (2)

The peanutclaw is under the control of its owner,
although it is not simple to control it, without specific training of the claw-controller, a part of the
limb that grows over the peanutclaw in the course of
the development of the limb. In other words, the more
peanutclaw moves, the larger the claw-controller grows.
The peanutclaw is supposed to crack peanuts and other
products, respectively to the owner wish, and it tastes
like a lobster.

However, the owner of the peanutclaw can switch off
the peanutclaw pushing on the middle of the claw-controller that makes the peanutclaw powerless for a minute. In such a way, the owner of the peanutclaw can use
the claw-controller to prevent the undesirable actions
of the peanutclaw.

In case of emergency, the claw-controller can para-
lyze the peanutclaw for a longer time and if the host
of the peanutclaw keeps pushing on the middle of the
claw-controller five times in a row, the claw-controler
holds the peanutclaw tightly for half an hour and the
peanutclaw, being deprived of the blood supply "dies"
and in a day the misbehaving separates from the body of
the host.

ASSIGNMENT 10: MY APOLOGY

Dear HomeworkRescue,

My professor has requested that I write an apology for my priapism during class. I don't know what "priapism" is, and I have no idea what I have done. This is all very upsetting to me. I am not good at apologies, and I just want all this trouble to go away. Please write a heartfelt apology for my "priapism" and if you could figure out what it is, please say how sorry I am for it.

Thank you.

Verñot Chumly

AN APOLOGY ON PRIAPISM

Respected Sir,

Please accept and understand my most sincere and serious letter of apology for the wrongdoing from me. I have felt from heart long and really hard about what happened and I realize how very emotionally upset you must have been.

It is the apology letter to you regarding my disease of priapism. That day I don't managed it in classroom, please realize my problem, it is the natural disease that's why I am suffering in it. Actually the disease is drug induced, injury related, or caused by infection, it is not sexual desire. In erection, the blood fills in penis and becomes erect. Though, unlike a normal erection that dissipates after sexual activity ends, the serious and persistent erection is sustained in the shaft (tube) of penis because the blood does not drain. The penile shaft remains very tough and hard and tip of the penis is soft. If it is not relieved on time, priapism can lead to permanent wounding of the penis and lack of ability to have a normal erection.

For many days, I am in very stress condition that what I say you in letter. I accept that what I did last week has hurt you a lot emotionally. This was totally my mistake. I don't know how I done it. It is fact sometimes I feel very abashment in the society. I promise you that it will never happen again and also hope that give me the forgiveness and opportunity to prove this to you.

I really know that it is very difficult for you to admit my sorry and apology but I hope that this apology letter will support me. I want to say to sorry and apology verbally, I will meet you after this week, and I hope that you will be able to give me forgiveness.

Your's sincerely

Mr. Veront Chumly

ASSIGNMENT 11: WHERE I SEE MYSELF IN 5 YEARS

Dear HomeworkRescue,

Great apology! Here's another assignment for you: My professor Mrs. Gulap has told the class to write an essay titled "Where I See Myself In 5 Years". Well, there's only one place I want to be 5 years from now: In her arms. Mrs. Gulap is so lovely I can barely take my eyes off her in order to cheat off the student sitting next to me. But I must! Mrs. Gulap is such an angel I almost feel guilty for stealing money from her purse whenever she limps out of the classroom to clean her colostomy bag. And this essay assignment is my opportunity to finally let her know how I feel.

I am positive that she gave us this assignment as a sneaky way to see if I'll make the first move and declare my love for her… the coy little tease. Its obvious that she feels the same way about me — you could cut the romantic tension between us with a knife. In fact, I've taken to bringing a knife to class and periodically flashing it at her to let her know that I know that she knows. She pretends to be shocked each time — its our little flirtatious game.

So please write the most beautifully seductive essay possible. The essay must say that in 5 years I see myself married to her with at least 9 beautiful children. Tell her I am enchanted by her long flowing auburn wig, smitten by her shapely hourglass head, and moved to amorous tears by her full, sensuous bee-stung nose.

Please write this essay with utmost care, as I really need an A and a wife.

Thanks guys!!!!

Verñot Chumly

"WHERE I SEE MYSELF IN FIVE YEARS"

Five years from now is a long time for anyone to be exactly sure about where they will be. Most will talk about work and their professional lives, while others will give details of how much money they desires to been accumulated. Personally, there is only one thing I know about that period, and that is that I want to be with you, in your arms.

Does it seem like a weird expectation seeing that I am your student? Well, it should not. You see, I knew you were the one the first time I laid an eye on you. Our subsequent meeting only confirmed that belief, as I was unable to take my eyes off you. Your beauty captivate, and makes me impossible for think about other things. My heart races every time I see you and feel I am melting into a small puddle on your feet.

I feel like I have fallen in love with an angel. Your beautiful face may well have been the creation of a God himself, and he certainly did his work in creating you. Your enchanting long flowing auburn wig captivates me, and repeatedly, I have to stop myself from running my hand down its lovely traces, to feel its sheer smoothness for the softness. Your shapely hourglass head is a reminder of exactly how exceptional you are, and seeing your full, sensuous bee-stung nose fills my heart with amorous tears. I cannot wait to spend the rest of my unique life with you.

So where do I see myself in five years? I think nine children will be sufficient to remind us of where we came, what obstacles we had to go through in order to reach where we are, and they will help us treasuring the beautiful love that we shared.

RE: ORDER 163512

Guys!!
Allow me to excerpt some of the comments scrawled in red pen on my paper when it was handed back to me the day after I turned it in:

"...How often I have caught myself, jolted and jerked at the last minute, having nearly drifted dreamily from my designated driving lane straight into oncoming traffic — distracted, enraptured, sweetly smitten with hot billowing mind blinding thoughts of your lips pressed so hard against mine that they come out the other side, reinvigorated and ready to take on the day like a rookie cop hopping sopping out of a steamy shower with his shoulder holster strapped on, locked, loaded and ready to rocket out of the back of my head..."

It goes on, dripping with passion's ooze right off the paper towards the floor, nearly ruining my suede *tip-tap* shoes. Only one problem —

It turns out that my teacher doesn't read or grade class papers herself. She makes Dustin, her Teacher's Assistant do it for her. And I regret to inform you that it is *this Dustin*, damn *Dustin* who has assumed that he was the target of the affection's arrow, which you so poetically fired from your quivering quill in my holy name.

He claims to have always felt this way about me too and that he never would have pressed hope against hope that his deepest yearns would be reciprocated. He is now convinced that he and I are in a committed relationship. All my rebuffs are laughed off as coy kittenish flirts. I can't shake this twerp. I just want to pass this class like gas.

I need you to break gently up with him for me in a new essay. Be tender, but brutal. I guess he thinks I am a *woman*. Can you somehow convince him that I am a man? (If it works, maybe I can use the argument on my parents)

Also (and this hurts the most), he gave me a C- on the paper. Let him know in the most oblique fashion that he won't get anywhere near my junk or *heart* for less than a B+. God, I'm so confused. Please help!!!

Verñot Chumly

It's Over Between Us

Thinking about where I will be in five years, only one thing makes sense. Each day I get convince that I really want to be in the arms of a sweet God given treasure in the heart of this one personality. Well, I must confess that my love makes me shiver every time our eye meet. My knees wobble; my heart race and I hate the feeling of that juice coming down from the depths of my belly. It makes me want to keep the urge alive all day and night. The thought of waiting five years is agonizing when we will discover the beautiful side of life. I simply cannot wait to see us make a big family of ten or eleven. The feeling is impeccable.

Who would challenge the Almighty that defined every curve and bump to make my bait the most beautiful creature I have ever seen under the sun? Craving and yearning for an ambitious woman of class is no easy thing to hide and that explains why I find you quite repulsive to my core. The law of magnetism vividly explains why we are not compatible, you are a man and so am I.

A man of my caliber will passionately pursue his prey and five years is long enough to entangle this woman in my breathtaking chest. I will do exactly that to spoil her with utmost love. Nevertheless, keep your dreams a live and do me one favour: keep off my path to success for this woman and grades mean everything to me.

ASSIGNMENT 12: CHILDHOOD EDUCATION
Knock-Knock U

Dear Kindsir or/and Foulmadame

Lets face it: the way that today's modern, go–for-broke, take-no-prisoners, hot-shot, accept-no-guff, step-off, don't-you-put-your-hands-on-me, I'll-knock-you-out-with-this-frozen-T-bone-steak, mess-with-me-and-I'll-pound-you-into-marinara, take-you-for-a-little-drive-and-pop-you-in-your-head, how-dare-you-threaten-me-I'm-descended-from-the-guy-who-played-knight-rider-I-mean-the-voice-of-the-car-not-the-male-human-lead children learn is through the power of something called "humor".

Please come up with SEVERAL humorous educational knock-knock jokes for to teach young children about EACH the following important topics:

1. **The Vietnam War** - The jokes must include hard facts about (a.) How many soldiers were killed (b.) How many were maimed (c.) The use of chemical weapons (d.) The effects of the war on families in the Nam.
2. **The Death Penalty in Texas** - The jokes must include facts about (a.) How many mentally disabled people have been put to death in the state (b.) How many men put to death turned out to be innocent, and (c.) How much fun it is to actually watch the penalty go down.
3. **Chlamydia** - Self-explanatory.

There is only one rule: No puns, no farts, no pee, no doo-doo and no mentions of Nixon. Make 'em funny!! Do it for the children!!

Thanks Guys!!!

Verp Churning

Childhood Education - Knock-Knock You

Vietnam War

Knock-Knock you!
Who's there?
Sing Chang Khu.
Sing what?
It's just my name, the name of the hero of the Vietnam War.

Knock-knock you!
Who's there?
It's me, Frank. Uncle Sam attempted to recruit me to par-
ticipate in the Vietnam War but I escaped and Uncle Sam still
can't find me.

The Death Penalty in Texas

Knock-Knock you!
Who's there?
Judge Dread, all criminals I had sentenced to death in Texas
were mad.

Knock-Knock you!
Who's there?
Can't remember my name. My doctor says I'm insane; but judges
in Texas says I should be sentenced to death and I don't even
understand what caused this mess.
Nevertheless, Judges in Texas are accustomed to sentence hundreds of people to death

Chlamydia

Knock-Knock you!
Who's there?
It's me, Chlamydia. I learn foreign languages. I speak well
using dictionary but without dictionary I am embarrassed to
say a word.

Knock-Knock you!
Who's there?
Chlomydia. I am enthusiastic and successful and I want to
teach children to be clever and good and my colleagues tell me
that I am a real Robbin Hood.

ASSIGNMENT 13: MEMORIES OF PET DUST

Dear AceEssaySolutions,

I am supposed to write an essay "describing the most fulfilling relationship I've ever had in my life". I can't do it because I am too overwhelmed with wistful tides of sloppy emotion. (Specifically, the emotion of not wanting to do my work myself.)

As a child, I yearned for a pet puppy, but alas, my father was allergic (to making me happy) and I myself was allergic to everything except dust. But one day, I read a book about puppies, which contained a very interesting fact: "after puppies die they decompose into dust."

I figured if I can't have a puppy, I can get the next best thing. I adopted a pile of dust from the friendly, baffled folks who ran the local pound. The dust and I were inseparable. Together we frolicked, romped and did everything that a boy does with a puppy, only I did it with a pile of dust.

Will you write up a series of specific adventures that we went on? They have slipped my mind (the dreaded Drink). I had a pet pile of dust.

Describe in detail:
1. The walks we took,
2. The tricks I taught him,
3. What I named it,
4. The dust puppies it had,
5. How I had to put it to death after it bit my grandmarm on the arm (it thought she was its tail).

Voight Chestadraw

MEMORIES OF PET DUST

If somebody would insist that relationships can only oc-
cur for living things, I beg to disagree. He was more than a
prey for vacuum cleaners in my mother's cozy and expensive
living room; a thing worth treating more than that of a crazy
nuisance. Dust: my best buddy. I know less about platonic love
or if it is even appropriate to describe the relationship I
had with my pet dust, especially that people made it exclusive
for them. One thing is for sure, my memories with my pet dust
will live on and would remain an inspiration to me.

If I can't have a puppy, then why not have the next best
thing? It may seem ridiculous but I couldn't find a way on how
to relief myself from such discontent. Sandburg, the name is
perfect for an impeccable pile of dust. We've shared adventures I could not possibly imagine I could do. We went to the
famous beaches in town and played hide and seek together. We
did not spare beach volleyball, with me as a loser for he had
an amazing talent in playing with ball games. I didn't have
a hard time training him to catch a ball using his nose, like
that of a seal in the Ocean Park. I could still remember the
way he wiggles his tail and licks my face as he successfully
caught the Frisbee. As jolly as he could be, it is unavoid-
able that he almost ended up hurting someone and the bad news
is, the victim was my grandmother. He bit her arm because he
thought she was his tail. She told my father about what happened and made my poor Sandburg homeless. My neighbor had a
female dog; almost like Sandburg's age. I began to notice
unusual actuation from Sandburg whenever Sissy and her owner
walk around the neighborhood. One night Sandburg escaped from
his cage and several months later, my neighbor told me that
Sissy was pregnant. She bore Sandburg six puppies namely: Ar-
thur, Lancelot, Galahad, Percevale, Lyonell, and Marianne.

Now, Sandburg is gone. Things come and go, that I know but
Sandburg will always be inside of my heart.

ASSIGNMENT 14: PRISON CORRESPONDENCE
Death Row Cheer-Up Letter

Peace In,

Every since the town zoo caught fire and closed up (couple days after I got my cool new lighter, hint-hint) there ain't nothing to do in my dumb old town so me and my boyz went on down to go hang out at the prison to cheer up the death row prizonors. We broke in pretty easy, but no matter how many times I done my famous impreshun of my aunt BooBoo as a dumb-assed chimp, none of the inmates laughed it up at me, they just tried to reach out and grab on my body and growl at me. This was not nearly as fun as it sounds. For some reason, that place was a real bum out. I got in trouble for busting into the prison and my punishment is that I gotta write a letter to all the prisoners on death row.

My best jokes and goofs didn't work on them, but I really wanna get these poor suckers to laugh. Please write a real funny letter to these dudes that will make them crack up with laughter so hard that every killer in the joint will forget their troubles and bust a gut from ear to ear.

Peace Out

Vorgan Chuchuski

A Letter to Death Row Inmates

Hi. I'm just a concern friend who deeply understand your predicament and wanted you to know, that I am feeling and sharing your pain. Bad as it seems, believe it or not, we are all destined to the same destination which is death. Unless of course we device a rocket for those who would want it otherwise; both to hell and heaven. Just like the judge, who after sentencing a felon to a death sentence did not reach his home or live long enough to witness the execution of the person he convicted, for he was hit by lightening. Heh heh.

I know at times we wish that the executioner would get a heart attack just before he pushes the button to see the look on their faces. It is good to know that, even those who sentence us now, have their judgments already been passed on them. I believe every one of you had a reason to do what you did. Hoping it was not just to get off the homeless streets. Maybe protecting a loved one, own self or defending your honor as few would understand it. What is important is would you do it again under same circumstance? If yes, you only did what you found prudent.

In a way, this could be a better death than a road accident, sudden death out of disease, being shot by robbers. My point being, these other deaths, happens suddenly and abruptly and without warning or time to reconcile with the one self. You know what they say about heaven, "lot of milk and honey," and the bees don't sting there.

Think about it.

RE: Letter To Death Row Inmates

Um, listen...

I sent your letter out to every death row prisoner in the state. And the verdict is... They loved it! Most of them told me (or implied) that it is worth being on death row just to have had a chance to receive such a well-honed piece of homespun humor. A lot of them are STILL "thinking about it." (get it?)

One prisoner (The *Larks County Slasher* — you might of heard of him, he famous!) was so moved that he sent me back a heartfelt 40 page letter that just said "Ha ha ha ha ha ha ha" repeated in shaky child's scrawl. It was darling. However: One prisoner was furious. He felt we were mocking him and belittling his situation. Here is the letter he wrote back to me:

Meat know you no write letter yourself. You tell Meat who did. Meat NEED know. Meat need name. Meat need address. Meat would love also Social Security number, but Meat not push Meat luck.
Love,
Thurston "Meat" Meatsbury, DDS.

So I just need your actual name and address so I can send it along to him. I have to warn you — I suspect the man is being coy, and that he is, in point of fact, sweet on you. You very well may be getting a big crunchy pile of kisses in the mail. Not too shabby.

Thanks!!

RE:RE: Letter To Death Row Inmates

Dear Customer,

We do not disclose any personal information, what for do you need writer's name and address?

Sincerely,
Victoria
Staff

RE:RE:RE: Letter To Death Row Inmates

Hi Victoria,

Thanks for providing me with your name. I sent it along to Meat. I think he was satisfied with the data, because in response he sent me a photo of him carving it into his arm with a makeshift shiv cobbled together prison style out of some soap suds, a couple socks, and an old discarded switchblade. It just says "Victoria" and underneath it says "SOOOON". On his other arm he carved a few doodles and phone messages for his cellmate.

I have been very happy with your work, Victoria and I have another assignment request. One of the other death row inmates (name of Taco "Keith" Stranglor) was asking if I could help him out with a little project. It seems Taco is due to be "put down" (to use the parlance of the pound) very soon and he needs to throw together some Last Words. (He'd cobble them together himself makeshift prison style, but I guess he's fresh out of soap suds and socks!)

Can you do it?

It should be simple. The poor guy just wants you to write the last words he shall utter in this world. If its not too much trouble. He needs it to sum up his entire life. And ultimately it ought to be the final definitive statement explicating All Of Life Itself. The state requires it can only be 25 words — no more, no less. He also told his cousin "Double Bean-Bean" that he would plug his chicken restaurant. Because, the thing is, they print your last words in the paper. And this guy, his cousin, needs the publicity or apparently his chicken spot might go out of business. So please compose some powerful parting words imploring mankind to savor every moment or something, but also be sure mention "Kracklin Bean Bean's Chick'n Spot off Route 9".

Thanks!

P.S. - If this works Taco may have you whip up some "first words" for his unborn son who is due to be squirted into the world the same day as his execution date. Crazy world, right? But I betcha that all ya'll nutz in the essay biz deal with this kinda stuff all the time.

Last Words Of Mr. Taco "Keith" Stranglor

Tried but world wouldn't let me fit in. Today could be a dad and partner at Kracklin Bean-Bean's Chicken Spot off route 9. Bye forever.

ASSIGNMENT 15: SLICK MARKETING
Slick Salesmanship

Dear BestEssaysFast,

Our professor insists: "a good salesman can sell anything!" For our mid-term we must write an upbeat TV commercial advertizing "human diarrhea" as a product. Include realistic selling points and sensible uses of human diarrhea. Make the average consumer excited about purchasing as much human diarrhea as he or she can get her hands on.

Let the sizzle sell the steak!

This particular steak being diarrhea!

Veno Chamore

Why Is Human Diarrhea What You Need?

In the nowadays world we are having more and more health problems, such as cancer, problems with breathing, etc. because of the toxic chemicals as we have to use them every day. Doctors say that there isn't any treatment to prevent the harm except to stop using any chemicals. And we all know that it is hardly possible. However, WE Have Found the treatment that can cure cancer, and even AIDS! It is "HUMAN DIARRHEA". Yes, but it works! Our scientists have created a special "Human diarrhea", that is hardly recognizable when comparing with the real one, thus, it is the original one, only with some special adding. So, our Human Diarrhea has the following advantages:

1) IT does help to cure cancer and Aids!!!
2) It looks nice(not as typical one) as it is in a blue color tablet
3) It smells wonderful due to special flower liquid
4) WE are the only one who sell it, so you won't buy any wrong one

As to the uses, we recommend to use our Human Diarrhea if:
·   You have cancer, Aids, or any dangerous disease.
·   You don't want to have these fatal diseases as Human Diarrhea helps prevent the appearance of any diseases.
·   You want to live longer as it rejuvenates you
·   You want to improve your general appearance.

Still think whether to buy it or not? Meanwhile, the others have already bought and not one package by the way, so, we may run out of it before you decide as the quantity is LIMITED.

ASSIGNMENT 16: POETRY OF SPITE

Dear EssayRescuers,

I told my professor I was going to get a tattoo that says "Mom" on my arm as a tribute to my lovely, wonderful mother. This was MY idea and I came up with it ON MY OWN. Then suddenly, he rolls up his sleeve and I see that HE has a tattoo on HIS arm that says "Mom", but HIS tattoo isn't referring to MY mom — it is referring (he claims) to HIS mom. Filthy thief.

And besides, I love my mom more than he loves his. But now if I get the same tattoo, I'm just an "unoriginal Joe" (I just made that phrase up — don't steal it). I gotta "raise the bar" (mine). I need to get something more special on my arm — (And I gots to beat that thieving weasel's tattoo — he's such a slimy sneak). Then all the sudden it hits me like a sack of wet tacos in the face — You write for me an elegant, erudite lyrical poetical tribute to my mom, and then I'll get the WHOLE POEM about my mom tattooed on my arm! Beat that!

Write a poem that talks about my mother and all she means to me. Make it really heartfelt. Bring up some of the special inside jokes me and mom share (just make some crap up)… mention how she used to wake me up by hitting me in the face with a sack of wet tacos… mention in the poem about how when she kissed me her little mustache would tickle — all over. Proofread your work cause I am taking it straight to the tat shop, and Mom is a stickler for grammer (mention it).

I Love You©

Veith Chilmer

Poetry of Spite

My love for my tremendous mom
I do believe will never wither
For many joyous years to come
Of sunny noons and gloomy blizzards
I will remember tickling hair
Of her moustache and loving kiss
I knew indeed how much she cared
To wake me up a way like this:
She hit me with a taco sack
With thorough tending, gentle touch
Who could do better grammar check?
My finest mommy, love you much!

ASSIGNMENT 17: LOGISTICS
Advanced Riddle Solvage

Dear TopAcePapers,

I signed up for a Logistics class because I truly love riddles, such as, "what was I thinking taking this horrible class?" A lot of the puzzlers in this course are harder than cracking open a bowling ball armed with just a slug, a balloon, a nose full of butter, and a can of wind. Lately we have been asked to solve some riddles that are rather personal and emotionally overwhelming for me. They just hit too close to home.

Here are the riddles I need you to solve:

1. You pluck the plumpest ripest orange from a tree in an orchard. The scent is glorious. Your yearning mouth is overcome by a tyranny of drool. You peel the orange. All there is inside the orange skin is a crammed assembly of severed human fingers. How did this come to pass?
2. You spend 15 days squatting over a pot of gold. Suddenly a thundercloud escapes from the zoo and applies for a job as a fry cook in a burger joint. How can this be rationally explained? (Hint: This really happened in 1974)
3. There is a wave of pure bliss that washes over all of humanity and lasts for infinity. What is the deal with that?
4. A gorilla wakes up in Mexico the back of a pickup truck with his paws duct taped to a donkey who is slathered in mustard. How many gallons of gas are in the gas tank?
5. If there was no such thing as death, what effect would this have on the raisin sales industry?
6. Why did my parents get divorced? Is it something I did?

Vodney Chascher

Logistics: Advanced Riddle Salvage

1. You pluck the plumpest ripest orange from a tree in an orchard. The scent is glorious. Your yearning mouth is overcome by a tyranny of drool. You peel the orange. All there is inside the orange skin is a crammed assembly of severed human fingers. How did this come to pass?

Take a piece in stick and in both hands the cut ends collectively your bent and thumbs index finger, covering the dough around your other finger to keep the hole open.

2. You spend 15 days squatting over a pot of gold. Suddenly a thundercloud escapes from the zoo and applies for a job as a fry cook in a burger joint. How can this be rationally explained? (Hint: This really happened in 1974)

15 days spent in a cooking class after that apply for cook job.

3. There is a wave of pure bliss that washes over all of humanity and lasts for infinity. What is the deal with that?

World should be like heaven or Eden. A pure feeling of goodness has turn a component of me that can exclusively be explained as world smiling back at me. I will accomplish full control by preceding the program.

4. A gorilla wakes up in Mexico the back of a pickup truck with his paws duct taped to a donkey who is slathered in mustard. How many gallons of gas are in the gas tank?

There is 10 gallons gas in the gas tank.

5. If there was no such thing as death, what effect would this have on the raisin sales industry?

Increase in sales because increase in population without decreasing individuals. Demand will increase with the increasing number of citizens.

6. Why did my parents get divorced? Is it something I did?

Due to misunderstandings parents get divorces, no there is noting you did.

ASSIGNMENT 18: MARKETING WITH ZAZZ!
Product Spin Off

Hey TermPaperSupport!!

I'm psyched!! I have an internship at the Global Corporate Headquarters of Silly String Industries in Detroit MI, and they have entrusted me with devising the marketing stratagem for their newest, most exciting product!! Detroit is an intensely bleak place!! But the good news is that we've figured out a way to make a quick, thick buck on the misery that pervades us!! It is called... "Somber String". Just as a can of Silly String makes any joyous celebration more exuberant, Somber String makes any depressing or traumatic experience more shocking, memorable, and profound. Here's what I need you to do:

1. Describe three (3) VERY somber occasions and how Somber String should be used in each of those situations. (NOT to cheer people up — that's not the point!)

2. Come up with 3 (three) fun and existentially interesting phrases to yell while spurting out a thick squirt of Somber String.

3. Somber String comes in three (3) (III) varieties: "Existential Dread", "Ennui Wee" and "So, So Suicidal". Describe the string of each of these varieties.

4. Describe realistic reactions of folks subjected to the Somber String experience.

5. Describe an incident where thick arcs of milky string soar across a lonely room to coat the face of a grieving person in the grip of a profound tragedy.

Thanks!!

Venal Checkum

PRODUCT SPIN OFF

There are bad times in every person's life. For awkward, un-pleasant and simply horrible moments in your life **Somber String** is a most suitable product to enhance such experiences!

Being ignored by people when trying to mingle with them. The most unfortunate incident revolving this: being bullied in high school. What makes this experience more horrible is that these experiences continued in the workplace and in other imperative set-tings such as family gatherings. It is so tempting to take out a **Somber String** can and squirt it on one's face as he/she weeps from being extremely depressed from this experience.

It is tempting to take out a **Somber String** can and squirt it on the face of the family members who are hurl the insults to make them wake up and realize what they are doing is wrong.

Being betrayed by relatives through financial means. It hurts so bad if the relatives swindle most of the funds, it makes it difficult to recover. Take out a **Somber String** can and squirt it on the face of the relatives when catching them by surprise of finding out the betrayal action that they did.

Phrase to yell out while squirting **Existential Dread Somber String**: *"I feel so scared to hope for a better tomorrow !"*. Phrase to yell out while squirting **Ennui Wee Somber String**: *"I can't feel there is a large potential of hope despite my dark ordeals!"* Phrase to yell out while squirting **So, So Suicidal Somber String**: *"I feel so hope-less and desperate, should I live or die?!"*

Existential Dread Somber String would be in black color. This dread has to be very dark due to the lack of hope this string poses. The smell would be similar to that of rotten food due to the severe gloominess felt. The string would be thick to describe the hovering dread it conveys.

Ennui Wee String would be light gray color. This string poses little hope in having things get better. The smell of this string would be that of salt. It would taste sour like a salty chip.

Suicidal Somber string would have to be in combination of black and gray. This is due to the severe bleak of hope it presents. The smell of this string would be similar to a skunk. The string would taste like a dead insect. The string would be so thick that it gags the mouth of the person from severe bleakness.

A person being so sad and depressed would be so irritated after being meanly squirted with **Somber String**. The sad and depressed person would probably retaliate by squirting **Somber Strings** back at them for a couple of minutes.

ASSIGNMENT 19: POP QUIZ
General Studies

Dearest AdvancedHomeworkPros,

I am taking a General Studies Class, and it is waaaay too general for me. (for I am a religious boy). We have a pop quiz that I need mad help with. Please answer these questions, reluctantly.

1. What is the meat of relief?

2. Why is it that only the good die young, choking on a mouthful of snicker doodles?

3. What do history scholars mean when they use the phrase "moisten the donkey"?

4. What is the opposite of this sentence?

5. Why did God make The Boy With The Upside Down Face?

6. What is the most shameful part of the human body?

7. What does it mean when one of the Great Philosophers smears gravy into his eyeballs?

Thanks a trillion and seven!

POP QUIZ: GENERAL STUDIES

(ANSWERS)

1. Meat of relief is meat which human get from slaughter animals on their holy Islamic day of year.

2. Good die young because Almighty Super nature being love good individuals therefore he call them in young.

3. moisten the donkey indicates means old families.

4. This is the opposite of this statement.

5. Conceive the risk of a right side world or what individuals in Northern hemispherical preconception call "right side up" being became upside down. Our Bible is full of accounts of folk as Mary, who had their world became upside-downt when they came face-to-face with God.

7. The most shameful part of the human body is fleshy part of the human body that individuals sit on.

8. Egg Eyeballs Formula is an amusing manner to serve treats. Whatsoever Halloween party will be fun on festive deals? Make your food look bang-up! Clothes it up and serve it! Your food table will spectacular with treats that look like Halloween Deviled Egg Eyeballs! Fun and festive this adds a special touch. They sample great fast and easy what else could you ask for!!

ASSIGNMENT 20: INTERPRETATION OF AN POEM

Dear TopGradeTermPapers,

Please write a lucid enlightening essay explaining precicely what on Earf this beautiful poem is about. Explore and explain the emotional resonance, the psychological insights and its place in the Western literary canon. Describe in detail the profound meaning of it.

Le Poem

Today the squishing of a queen bee was hand sewn
To the bra of mankind's ache
And archery lessons cost more than
Disco snot, frozen in the shape of your stupid.
Did anyone ever take a class to learn how to chew carrots?
They did? Who? Was it Josh? I never trusted that guy.
Have you seen
The way
He giggles when I cry?
I heard he once tongue kissed a cat
Oh hey
I didn't
See you there Josh.
How long have
You been standing
Behind me?
A great ship comes climbing over the mountain of your
Facial acne
And yes
Oh yessssss
Even
your bacne
peace out

INTERPRETATION OF AN POEM

This poem can be characterized as a representation of postmodern poetry. First, it is its exceptional form that attracts the reader that reminds English letter 'F'. This can be some particular sign or symbol (fall, failure, future, fool, etc.) created by the poet or it can be mere a coincidence of reader's interpretation and author's literary invention.

The poem is autobiographic revealing the truth of author's thoughts, feeling, and perceptions of the world. There is a complex interplay of a language, and exploratation of the shelf, as content of form.

Expression of reality the reader encounters in the poem is about everything and nothing and only the sixth line (*They did? Who? Was it Josh? I never trusted that guy*) is referring to a particular person, who had done something which realized in author's lack of trust to Josh. Giggling when someone cries is called indifferences if not worse. It is clear to the reader that the author has suffered some negative experience.

However, unexpectedly there he is, Josh. This person really means a lot to the author of the poem. The line, *I heard he once tongue kissed a cat*, is like a reminiscence about some bright memorable fact.

Or, it can refer to facial acne which has just appeared. In the next line the expression 'Oh yessssss' can be also a signifier of various feelings such as either a relief, or frustration of the author or authors.

It is quite clear that this poem has the same characteristics like the most of the post-modernistic poems have. The ideas and thoughts are expressed though a flow of consciousness. Finally, as any literary work, this post-modernistic poem is unique.

RE: Interpretation Of An Poem

Oh My god You Guys…

It turns out my PROFESSOR is the one who wrote that Le Poem. He is very insulted that you said it was like an "F" for "failure" and "fool". Right now he is sobbing and screeching that he won't come out from under his desk until he sees a revision of the assignment that gives his Le Poem much grander praise and declares it to be one of the finest poems ever written by a human man.

I think the thing that hurt him most was your little "F" crack (though I thought it was a funny insult — he is being a big assed baby if you ask me…) Anyway, what you need to do to get me an A is to write your response in the shape of the letter "A". That is the only thing that will undo all the horrible damage you've horribly done.

If you don't do this, he said he'd kick me out of school and then he'd try to get me sent to prison jail. Please ASAMFP, before he runs out of food under his desk and I have a damn corpse on my hands. (gross!)

Thanks!! and APFMBMFR!!!

RE:RE: Interpretation Of An Poem

Dear Student,

the revised paper is in the attachment.
The poem is indeed very specific and it's meaning is
not clear. For this reason, it is difficult to make
better analysis (no background information about the
author, no time period identified etc).

If this poem has been written by your professor it
really explains some things...

Hope you will passing this course!

Kind regards,

Writer Malcolm

REINTERPRETATION OF LE POEM

This beautiful poem, full of
deep emotional resonance and
psychological insights, tells the
reader about author's perception of
the world. There is complex interplay
of language, as form of expression, and
presentation of the self, as content of
form.

The author starts with a philosophic
reflection about the mankind's ache, to
communicate his emotional state. From
the first look, it seems this reflection is
hidden under the mask of incoherent words, but
deep inside the author feels the imperfection of
our world and develops this thought by stressing
the vapidity of the modern society devoted to the
modern forms of entertainment such as disco and
figuratively comparing it with other activities.
Archery lessons represent entertainment activities,
which contribute to spirituaval advance of the "shot",

but they require more   effort and time. It is
much easier to go   to the disco and have
some fun, then do   something more meaningful.
In modern society,   youth is not committed to
spiritual advance and   enhancement of the cultural
level. The author   sees the outcomes of such
ignorance lead to the   degradation of society.

     The author   questions "…Did
anyone ever take   a class to learn how
to chew carrots?"   just to emphasize that
simple things do   not require training.
Suddenly, the   author's thoughts
became riveted to   Josh, having extremely
negative attitude   to this person.
Sometime ago Josh   might   used to be a friend
or lover of the   author, but the things changed! And
therefore, this person   excites so mixed emotions of the
author: offence ("…   he giggles when I cry?"), anger ("…ship
climbing over the mountain of your facial acne"), contempt ("…I never
trusted that guy") and defiance ("…he once tongue kissed a cat").
This insight proves that love is one step away from hate.

   Obviously, the author gives vent to his anger, frustration and
indignation and pours out all emotions on Josh. In some sense, Josh
comes as a relief for the inflamed mind of the author ("…and yes oh
yessssss"). This insight   embodies emotional
release and abstraction from   problem
   This poem has the same   characteristics like
the most of the post-modernistic   poems have. The
author pays more attention   to the content,
emotional resonance and   psychological
insights rather than to   rhyming. Finally,
as any literary work, this   post-modernistic
poem is unique and with   exceptionally
profound meaning.

ASSIGNMENT 21: ROAST A DEAD DEER MOUSE

Dear TermPaperPal,

I am a class clown. I posses that "special something" that makes folks bust a gut. No matter the situation, I come out with a perfect one liner.

Example: yesterday I got in trouble for insulting a moronical kid in my Extremely Remedial Reading class. It wasn't a big deal. I just stared at him for a full minute thinking up a good one, then I said, "kid, you have the charisma of a dead deer mouse". I can't help myself — I just have the gift of wit when I am in the zone. But my teacher got really mad and told me that it wasn't nice.

So then I turn to my teacher and I really got her good. I looked her dead in the eye for ten minutes, then said "you have the charisma of a dead deer mouse." See? It's in my blood. I got elephantitis of the funny bone. She couldn't resist laughing, but to save face she pretended to be yelling at me to go to the principal's office — and when I got there, the principal said he was real disappointed in me.

At this point, all of my class clown training kicked in and I looked Principal Dilmore dead in the eye for a good half hour then I said, "you have the charisma of a dead deer mouse". He asked me what I had against dead deer mice and I said, "Everything…" I searched for the words as I absently wiped some soup from my hair. "Shoot, I could do a whole insult routine roasting a dead deer mouse."

He said, "OK. Then that is your punishment. You will go up to the podium in front of the whole school and you will unleash a snappy tirade of brutal insults against a dead deer mouse. This will get it all out of your system. I will provide the dead deer mouse. You provide the litany of devastating material."

Well… suddenly I can't think of any jokes. So I need you to come up with ten really funny insults against a dead deer mouse. (Only advice I can give you — maybe go after the charisma of the thing.) Please make it witty, sharp and hilarious. That'll show them. That'll show everyone.

Villiam Choomer

ROAST A DEAD DEER MOUSE

Hey, did you all know buddy that the deer mouse be-
longed to the genus of Peromyscus? Hmmmm,… even I did
not know that until now when my pal gave me this information.
He said –'Hey Johnny' you know why these rodents are
called deer mice? And I said no buddy, go ahead and tell
me.
So he says – cos' they are as agile as deer themselves!
And I said – 'You know what? We gotta avoid them like
the plague, cos' we don't want no creepy, crawly, dirty,
stinky deer mouse jumpin' at us when we are celebrating
'trick or treat on Halloween'!!!!

And you know what pal? I sayz 'What'?
They must have made good their escape from Noah's Ark a
couple of centuries ago!!!! It must have been like – Hey!
North and South America, here I come!!!!
And that's not all!!!
Oh yeah? Go on…tell me….anything interesting?
Yeah….these deer mice are the carriers of the 'hantavi-
rus' very harmful to us humans…

So that's it….I get it buddy….so mice deer are a dangerous species!!!! Can I say something really nasty about
them?
Please…go ahead….tell them all you want….nasty little
creatures–

a)   These puny little deer mice with their socksy feet,
think they are like Cinderella dancing and prancing about
with Prince Charming….I'll show them!.... I'll get them
if it's the last thing I do before I die!!!

b)   These deer mice can go to hell for all I care….I
don't care a penny if they came from Noah's Ark! I will
shoot down these beady – eyed, furry balls of hair like
no man's business and make a punching bag out of them.

c)   My advance wishes to them would be – 'May their
souls rest in peace'!!!

RE: ORDER 75412

OK guys,

I stood at the podium reading that entire soggy tirade with all the
enthusiasm I could scare up. By the time I finished, every person in the
auditorium had been bored into a deep snoring sleep, including me.
They tried hard to wake me — they poked me with sticks, dunked my
head in the toilet... they took humiliating pictures of my sleeping body
with several dead deer mice stuffed in my mouth, they spat and laughed
in my fat face. Nothing worked.

When I finally woke up, my principal said that my roast had contained
only 5.7 jokes. That means there are 4.3 more jokes due to fulfill the full
ten (10) I (you) was (were) asked (paid) to write.

Principal wants the remaining 4.3 jokes to consist of:
• 2 knock-knock jokes,
• 1 witty limerick, and
• 1.3 fart jokes

And remember: all these insults should be as clever and hilarious as a
sucker punch to the face of a dead deer mouse.

Dead Deer Mouse Roast

Jokes

What do you call a deer with no eyes - No idea
What do you call a deer with no eyes and no legs - Still no idea.
What do you call a mouse deer with no limbs or senses? Dead mouse deer!!!!

Limerick

There was once a mouse deer who jumped into bed
He fell on his crown and broke his fat head
The butcher, the baker tried hard to mend
But the mouse deer's life had come to an end!!!!

Fart Joke

Paul: Did you go deep into the forest?
Ernie: Yeah buddy, where no man has ever been.
Paul: Did you come across any wild animals?
Ernie: OMG!!! I came face to face with a terrifying lion!
Paul: Did it scare the shit outta you?
Ernie: Yup, but I knew what steps to take.
Paul: What steps?
Ernie: Long ones - I ran to the nearest tree and climbed it.
Paul: Oh! And what about the little mouse deer you always carried?
Ernie: Oh the foolish thing just jumped from my hand into the damn lion's mouth.
Paul: Did you try to shoot it?
Ernie: I tried but I couldn't.
Paul: Why what's your problem man?
Ernie: I ran out of film.
Paul: Then did you get down from the tree?
Ernie: No, you only get down from a swan but wood from a tree.
Paul: Buddy, your answers stink worse than a mouse deer fart.

ASSIGNMENT 22: PRISON CORRESPONDENCE 2

Essay To End The Death Penalty Once & For All

Dear HomeworkAssist,

Welp, I really backed my hiney into a sticky willy this time. This guy Meat who's kinda my prison pen pal slash slasher keeps sending me letters that say *"Meat gon kut u if u no help Meat"* scrawled over and over in red crayon. I am afraid this might start to get a little creepy, so I promised Meat I could get him off of death row. Meat wrote back *"u gots to b yanking my nugget"*. I'm NOT!

All I have to do is write a letter to the prison warden that convinces him that the death penalty is wrong and that I am not yanking his nugget even an inch. If the warden thinks I am just yanking his nugget... there IS a TINY chance that he WON'T shut down death row forever.

Can you write a essay vehement and passionate enough to convince the warden to shut down death row? Be VERY careful in EVERY sentence to make it VERY clear that I "AIN'T yanking his nugget". Explain in the essay (in EVERY SENTENCE) that I would not and could not yank his nugget on this sensitive and nuanced issue.

My Meat is in your hands.

Vorgan Chuchuski

Essay Eliminating the Death Penalty

The argument regarding death penalty hinges on whether it is just or not for most people, and I aint yanking your nugget. There are many crimes that if each of us were involved in or witness's too would seem to justify the use of death penalty, and I aint yanking your nugget. However, the state or government is an entity and while it is meant to represent the individuals that reside within its borders it often pursues a course that is not meant to deal true justice, and I aint yanking your nugget. Each of us has the option to defend ourselves and do so in justified, legal and ethical ways, and I aint yanking your nugget. The state however, has no need or desire to defend us as individuals, and in fact centers on the expedient adjudication of events which in many cases results in plea bargains and injustice, and I aint yanking your nugget.

According to Death Penalty Info.org; "As of October 27, 2010 there have been 138 exonerations in 26 different States, since 1973" (Death Penalty Information Center), and I aint yanking your nugget. Some have estimated that between 2-5% of the persons sentenced and put to death are innocent of the charges against them, and I aint yanking your nugget. However, even though innocent people are put to death, and the state has ulterior goals in the end it comes down to the taking of a human life for no better reason than an eye for an eye, and I aint yanking your nugget.

Works Cited

Death Penalty Information Center,. "Innocence and the death penalty."

2010: n. page. Web. 23 Nov. 2011. <http://www.deathpenalty-info.org/innocence-and-death-penalty>

ASSIGNMENT 23: THE STINK OF CHOICE, OR STANDING AND RANKING

(Evaluative Status As It Relates To Value Judgement At Large)

Dear MidtermRescue,

As I have elected to attain a black belt masters degree in Pseudo-Psycho Critical Delineation, this is a required course for me. But I am precisely the least judgmental person I have ever met. So, this is not only the #1 worst class I have ever taken, but it is the #2 worst class ever taught in the history of education. The only good part is that my professor doesn't believe in grades, so it is Pass/Fail. I can't bear to do this assignment myself as I find the very premise morally reprehensible. Do it for me please, thank you!!

1. Rank the top <u>8 Major Races</u> (Asian, Latin, European, Native, Eastern European, Black African, East Australian, and Other) in numerical order from greatest to worst providing a one sentence reason for each placement.

2. Rank man's proven Prophets in order on a numerical scale <u>from most holy to not holy at all</u>: (Jesus, Buddha, Shiva, Garvin, Mohammed, L. Ron Hubbard, Joseph Smith) Give a reason for each position.

3. Rank these <u>5 fatal diseases</u> in order of fun with number 1 being the most fun and number 5 being only a little bit fun. AIDS, Cancer, Heart Disease, Ebola, Pechuco, and Emphysema. No reasons required, just cold numbers.

STINK OF CHOICE

The 8 major races, ranked in order greatest to least greatest

1. **Latin** – I chose Latin as the greatest because Latinos have brought the world great leaders, social justice advocates, food, fashion, quinceaneras, and dance.

2. **Australian** – Australians are second because they started as an island of misfits and criminals yet became a significant influence in the world, and Australia has produced some of the world's greatest actors.

3. **Black African** – The black race came in third because of the rich heritage, music, food, dance, and fashion; they have contributed a great deal too modern society including the civil rights movement and a wide variety of great leaders.

4. **European** – Western European came in fourth because of the vast number cultures and traditions they have brought.

5. **Asian** – Asian ranked in the middle because they have offered the world great advancements in technology, despite the questionable food and humanity issues in many Asian countries.

6. **Native** – I ranked native sixth because the modern world has swallowed up a lot of native culture.

7. **Eastern European** – I do not know that much about Eastern European people, which leads me to assume they have not contributed that much.

8. **Other** – Other came in last because I'm not really sure who would be included in other, so I couldn't defend ranking them over any other race.

Rank man's prophets from most holy to least holy

1. **Jesus** – Jesus came in first because I believe in the Christian faith, and I believe he is the most holy of leaders.

2. **Buddha** – Buddha has provided generations with the divine power of introspection and peace.

3. **Shiva** – Although I don't believe in the power of Shiva, I believe she is more holy than the rest of the people on this list.

4. **Mohammed** – Mohammed has a rich cultural history, which adds to his overall "holiness" because it enhances his character.

5. **Joseph Smith** – I seriously question the validity of Joseph Smith's visions.

6. **Garvin** – I don't know who this is, yet I am willing to believe he has greater insight into life than L. Ron Hubbard.

7. **L. Ron Hubbard** – L. Ron Hubbard is last because he is a novelist, and I do not believe he has any additional insight to the human experience or the divine than the average man walking down the street.

Five diseases ranked by most fun

1. Cancer
2. Heart Disease
3. Emphysema
4. Ebola
5. Pechuco
6. AIDS

RE: #178614-SOC

Dearest Sir or Madame,

Great job!! Amazing work!! Your ranking of diseases by degree of funTASTICness is eerily dead on — Trust me, I found out the hard way (inside my body).

I just need a few very teeny, VERY FREE revisions:

1. I am a deeply religious Scientologist and I was so repulsed by your baseless slander of my faith that I threw up for hours and hours and hou- (excuse me... I'll be right back... I have to run into the bathroom and throw up some more, just as soon as I finish typing this explanation of why I stopped typing the word "hours" before I managed to get to the "r" portion of the word.) So please put my fine faith on the top of the list (or else they'll destroy me).

2. I find Mr. Jesus H. Christ to be vile. Please drop him to last place. Just explain that he is "totally grody" and that I find it disgusting that his so-called "teachings" don't even rhyme.

3. My sister is a devout follower of Garvin (he even touched her one time, in a crowded elevator) so I need you to put him at around 2 or 3.

4. My professor is a proud Eastern European (she has a neck tat that says "Eastern European People Rulez 4-Eva!") so please make Eastern Europe higher up on the list. Also her ex-husband is a Latin Type and she really hates him, so please drop the grubby, two-faced Latins down below "Other" and below a new racial category called "Cheatin' Cretins".

5. Also if you could please dial down your intense racism by at least 11 percent, I think this would make my professor feel very garvin.

Thanks!!

The 8 major races, ranked in order greatest to least greatest

1.   **Eastern European** – Eastern European is clearly the greatest race because of their intense intellect, talent and contributions to the world.
2.   **Australian** – Australians are second because they have managed to not only survive, but thrive on an island filled with many of the world's most dangerous spiders and snakes.
3.   **Black African** – The black race came in third because of the rich heritage, music, food, dance, and fashion; they have contributed a great deal too modern society including the civil rights movement and a wide variety of great leaders.
4.   **European** – Western European came in fourth because of the vast number cultures and traditions they have brought.
5.   **Asian** – Asian ranked in the middle because they have offered the world great advancements in technology.
6.   **Native** – I ranked native sixth because the modern world has swallowed up a lot of native culture.
7.   **Other** – "other" encompasses a great number of people, who have likely contributed a great deal to the world.
8.   **Latin** – Latinos are last because they are liars and cheaters.

Rank man's prophets from most holy to least holy

1.   **L. Ron Hubbard** – I am a devout Scientologist and I believe L. Ron Hubbard is most holy.
2.   **Garvin** – Next to L. Ron Hubbard, Garvin is the greatest spiritual leader and has divine insight into the human condition.
3.   **Buddha** – Buddha has provided generations with the divine power of introspection and peace.
4.   **Shiva** – Although I don't personal believe in the power of Shiva, she is as great spiritual leader within the Hindu faith.
5.   **Mohammed** – Mohammed has a rich cultural history, which adds to his overall "holiness" because it enhances his character.
6.   **Joseph Smith** – I seriously question the validity of Joseph Smith's visions, but I have no proof they weren't valid.
7.   **Moses** – Moses is second to least because I do not believe he was a holy man at all.
8.   **Jesus** – Jesus is last on the list because he is vile, his tactics are grotesque, and I think its disgusting the way his terrible "teachings" do not rhyme.

ASSIGNMENT 24: DEVELOP A NEW "SOUL BROTHER" HANDSHAKE

Dear A-PlusPapers,

Recently, I decided to quit my yappin' & complainin', and to cease my hollerin' & howlin' about my fussin' & yammeratin' (with regard to my acute apprehensions towards the United States Government) and dang ol' DO somethin' 'bout it. I resolved to finally step up to the money plate and put my feet where my mouth is pulling up my own ass up by it's bootstraps. You guessed it — I'm runnin' fer the highest office in the land: Mayor of Vittleton, Arkansass.

My campaign *was* sailin' smoooooth as balls (shaved), but the other day as I was out shaking hands tryna scare up votes, I had a scare of my own — I seen a black guy. Just standing there on the street, black as rice (we serve only rotten rice here in Vittleton). Word at the police station is that the Black just moved here. Now if I wanna git his vote I'm a gonna need to shake his black hand. But I don't know any soul brother handshakes. My standard handshake is comprised of merely two parts:

1. Flatten hand, wipe sweat and human seed from palm onto pants then grasp the other fellers hand, pumping thrice.

2. Let go, in order to wipe sweat and seed from palm onto pants again.

As much as I believe in that traditional handshake (as taught to me by my papa when I was still in my mama's belly), I need to win this black guy over to lock in the black vote. And, the only thing I know about black guys is that they like their handshakes complicated, with a whole honkin' heap o' palm-flaps, wrist-twists, fingerflips and switch'em ups.

I need ya'll to think up for me an original, exciting, flamboyant 12 part soul brother handshake that'll knock that proud voter right onto his big black ass. Spell it out for me step by step — use drawings and careful descriptions. The future of Vittleton is in my hands, and how they move. I hereby put my movement in your hands.

Vlumpy Custered

SOUL BROTHER HANDSHAKE

The soul brother handshake is universal. Putting myself in her shoes, it must be amazing to watch two men, from different continents, who can barely communicate with one another, easily slip into the familiar, rhythmic slaps (Brooks, 2005). To many who like a handshake, they refer to it as a ritual of grasping each other's hand and in most cases accompanied by a brief up and down of the grasped hands with greetings such as, ''How are you?''

The initial stage a ''Soul Brother'' handshake is to slap palms together, followed by movement of fingers and lastly, close up fingers together in a half grip. This is how real brothers make the acquaintance of each other.

During a campaign process, ''Soul Brother'' handshake speak volumes to electorate, especially when a candidate freely initiate a handshake. It conveys a level of trust, balance and equality. One should be free to extend a handshake to people except where health and cultural issues dictate otherwise; Muslim women are not permitted to greet one hand by hand. On the other hand, trying to execute a handshake while wearing gloves is viewed unsuitable.

When contesting for a high office in the land such as Mayor Position in Vittleton, Arkansas, one should understand when and how to do it. Under doing a handshake leaves the other party unsatisfied and may refer to you as a proud person whereas over doing it is also bad because it may make one uncomfortable (Brooks, 2005).

Reference
Brooks, J. S. (2005). Brother in the bush: an African American's search for self in East Africa. Berkeley: Agate Publishing

ASSIGNMENT 25: ETYMOLOGICAL SOURCEAGE
Slang Origins

Dearest A1EssayAssist,

I signed up for a class in "Etymology" because I have literally had a life-long love affair with insects. As a tot, my mommy walked in on me making out with my praying mantis about, oh, a hundred times! Well, imagine my horror when, 6 weeks into this course I suddenly realized — "etymology" means *'the frickin' study of the origin of words and phrases'*. I was thinking of *entomology*. The dang classroom was so filled with flesh flies every week, anyone could've made the same mistake. (I'm in Arkansas)

Well now I got all these stupid assignments about the origin of slang expressions, and I sure as Zeus's tube top ain't gonna do them. Enter you. Assignment:

You are given 3 brand new slang phrases and their meanings. These phrases are so new, they have yet to appear in print or the internet. Your research job is to track down the true story of how each phrase came to be.

PHRASES:

1. **"Let's funk a jackal to def"** - *this means 'lets eat some yogurt'.*

2. **"That wasp's wrist is the hornet's elbow"** — *this is what you say when you find your feline's sleeping garments to be the cat's pajamas.*

3. **"Knock back a shiny taco's lip"** – *this means 'to accidentally discover that your little sister is in fact made from tinfoil.*

Using old-fashioned detective work, find and explain the source of each phrase. The provide a sentence that uses each phrase in a pat, yet strangely life-changing statement.

And don't forget to slip the old wet hoedown a ticklin's brownie blower. Thanks!!

Vang Chymsle

ETYMOLOGICAL SOURCEAGE: "SLANG ORIGINS"

"Let's funk a jackal to def"- let's eat some yogurt.

From early 21st century Brazil. An American scientist in Brazil observing jackals when he discovered a jackals eating bad smelling yoghurt which he had thrown out of his house. When scientist came back and related the story, his children started using the phrase whenever they were forced to eat yoghurt. "Since we are on a diet lets funk a jakcal to def."

"That wasp's wrist is the hornet's elbow"-this is what you say when you find your feline's sleeping garments to be the cat's pajamas.

From a researcher studying insects. A French researcher got confused between the anatomy of hornet and wasp due to wrong equipment. The colleagues when discovered the blunder started joking about how such confusion could have taken place and to describe the situation compared it to becoming confused about one's cat. This evolved into its current state when one of the scientist's kid made the dog wear the cat's pajamas. "After a lot of howling from our dog I found the reason for it was that the wasp's wrist was the hornet's elbow."

"Knock back a shiny taco's lip" - to accidentally discover that your little sister is in fact made from tinfoil

From a customer eating a plastic taco. A customer became the brunt of April fool's day when he accidently ate a plastic taco. When the joke was revealed the customer was embarrassed. This was related to the incident of an alien where a brother while warming food discover his sister made of tin foil. "Upon burning the toe of my sister I knocked back a shiny taco's lip."

RE: Assignment no. 79814AL S

Dearest A1EssayAssist,

Your slang expertise dribbled my garage meat into a porcelain corn chip's rowboat! However, I do have one growling flasher to pick with you. Your neo-coyote miserygasm may have fainted in paint, but the last punt of your warbler spleen trout groin didn't make a lick of sense. Could you whisper tutus into a pot of bacon for me? It shouldn't take 3 horsey sauce chimichangas more than a hellhound's yellow yawn, but it would mean the Schindler's hiney to me and my little vasectomy defyers.

Grule You Very Much!

Vang Chymsle

Re: RE: Assignment no. 79814AL S

Client,

Is it possible clarifying your request? Would you
like to submit for a revision of the essay?

Thank you,

A1EssayAssist

RE: Re: RE: Assignment no. 79814AL S

Dear Madame,

Terribly sorry gents, I'm afraid you've lost me. I have no clown pudding what you're talking about. I'm not sure if you're showing off, or just farting up a walrus's windpipe, but either way I don't think I can hang beef with the Big $heboygan of slang. Guess I'll have to grease my own tuba with the fruit my papa shipped me. This will likely do extensive damage to my tuba. I assume you have a standard reimbursement policy for these situations.

Rolfing hurts,

Vang Chymsle

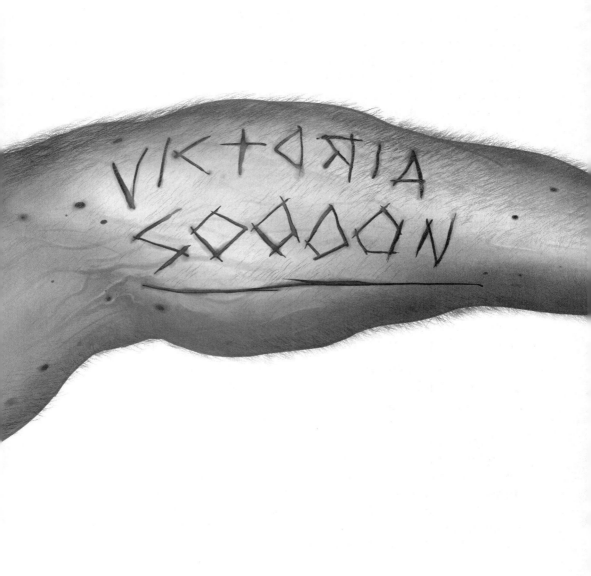

ASSIGNMENT 26: MYTHOLOGY AND MORAL

Read each traditional myth with a critical eye. Then answer questions:

A Lithuanian Fairy Tale:

A Prince falls asleep while reading this story, and wakes up with a cup of fruit salad delicately balanced on his forehead. He stands, and the fruit scatters. When the Prince (who once shaved a llama clean so he could tattoo a walrus on its tummy) tries to pick up the pieces, he notices that the fruit is covered in pimples, and that his hands are now lobster claws. When he squeezes the fruit zits, he vomits a rainbow. The rainbow breast-feeds a hog until it is plump enough to slaughter for lunch. Yum.

1. What is the point and the moral of this story?
2. Describe something like this that has happened to you recently.
3. Was the walrus happy? How could you possibly know that?

A Yanomamo Creation Myth:

Two stars high up in the sky begin a casual conversation (out of boredom more than anything). One of the stars asks if the other one knows any good Jew jokes. The other responds, quite devilishly, "Fuck me, I don't even know any jews." This is how hurricanes were invented.

1. What is the point of this story? What is the moral?
2. Do you know any jews? Explain yourself.
3. When will humanity learn?

An Irish Fable:

A daddy potato walks in on his son selling his vote to a fish. Incensed, the hippie paternal spud furiously puts his cigar out on the child 61 times, in the shape of the words "sorry, boy". Just then, Zeus walks in and explains that he has had his skin replaced by tongues. When questioned on this, Zeus says he lost a bet, and then dives headfirst down a Slip N' Slide moistened with nougat and salted to taste.

1. What is the point of this story? What is the moral?
2. What is the point of your own life? (3 words or less — no cursing)
3. If you could pour hot lava down the front of your father's pants or down the back of his pants which would you choose and why?

FAIRY TALES ANSWERS

LITHUANIAN FAIRY TALE

The main point of this story is we can not degrade anything, as every thing has indispensability as in this story, fruits make the King in the state of Stigma.

Describe something like this that has happened to you recently.
I know a person who is not good in mathematics and, our class can bet he can not pass the paper of mathematics, but he didn't even pass the paper but get the highest marks in it as well.

You think the walrus was happy? How could you possibly know that?
Walrus was happy because he has potential to tackle from any challenges as he tackle with the little foes.

YANOMAMO CREATION MYTH

The moral of the story is to "Mind your own business" and we should not put our leg in the matter of other.

Do you know any jews? Explain yourself.
No! I don't know any Jews yet, and I am a person who does not believe on all such things. Every religion has good and bad people in it, but we can not accuse the whole community due to that single person.

When will humanity learn?
The main problem, which we have faced from last few years is the lack of knowledge among our elders. We need preachers to educate us and until that time comes people should learned what humanity is?

AN IRISH FABLE

The main point of the story is don't even think evil for the others as it will harm you as well.

What is the point of your own life? (3 words or less — and no cursing)
Become the Best.

If you could pour hot lava down the front of your father's pants or down the back of his pants which would you choose and why?
I don't want to hurt my father.

ASSIGNMENT 27: TEACHING LEARNING: A EDUCATIONAL SONG

Dear TopRankEssays,

As you may know, little kids are not smart. They simply have no worthwhile knowledge in them. So they need help learning all the facts that us adults are smart enough to already know. Are you following me? Good. In my class, we have to come up with a song that is a "pneumonic device" to teach children, so that they will not be so blooming ignorant.

You must come up with new lyrics to the tune of "Twinkle, Twinkle Little Star" that details the atrocities and torture that have gone on at Abu Ghraib Prison.

Include at least 8 relevant facts in the lyrics and include graphic specifics. The sweet song must be so informative that when the toddler gets done singing the little ditty, he or she will be a leading expert on the topic of the barbaric horror of Abu Ghraib.

Vashti Chunyan

Educational Rhythmical Song

Fear And Evilness
(to the tune of Twinkle Twinkle Little Star)

I eat my breakfast,
Afraid I would get attacked,
American soldiers give me suddenly pain,
I don't feel I gain it.

I went in another direction,
My condition just gives me pain also in this Arab prison.
Not realizing the punches I get,
Hitting me one by one from the get go.

All I do is hit people with kindness,
I don't deserve all this evilness.
It's a big wonder if this is a big punishment,
I live life with big resentment.

I asked God of the reason He has made me suffer,
But all I get is an answer of nothing.
I started worshipping all of the Gods,
Eating food for the gods every day.

Everyday holds no safety,
For I am in danger daily,

To kill me and chop me,
Pieces by pieces I get broken,
No way will I ever get unbroken.
Asking people to help please,
Please oh please but nobody does.

ASSIGNMENT 28: REVERSE ANALYSIS

Reverse Dream Analysis

I am dope at analyzing dreams. I can suffuse any dream object or action with enough symbolic power to make the dreamer re-evaluate his life and leap shattered from a skyscraper into the drooling jowls of a wood chipper. I've done it like 8 times, but whatevs.

Our class assignment is to document 3 of our own dreams and provide self-analysis. Only one problem: I don't dream. Ever. The closest I came to dreaming was once when I was 7, the vague translucent image of a bowl of oranges flashed in my mind's eye for 10 seconds and then scampered away forever without leaving so much as a receipt.

I don't want to cheat at this, but my bouncy newborn (wife) has got to eat, so this is what I propose — I will provide you with the *analysis* and you guys just fill in a dream that would fit that interpretation. Make sure that each dream you make up is a startlingly riveting visionary psychosexual feast that matches my masterful evaluation of it.

Analysis of Dream 1: "*This was a strange dream. My mother's three heads illuminated how time melts like caramel down a camel's hump. When each balloon popped, the sound of a lie came out of it because thats what happens when bodies start slapping.*"

Analysis of Dream 2: "*This is a recurring dream of mine. The marmalade clearly stands for 'Science'. The actions in this dream represent my dude-quest for 'brocial justice' to prevail even as God (the walls) snorted all 500 mosquitoes up into His nose. I don't know why those badgers in the dream got clumps of Science all over their thighs, but the twist ending was amazing! I totally did not see that coming, but it tied everything together perfectly.*"

Analysis of Dream 3: "*I don't know if I should be forthright about what this means, Mrs. Kenmare, as it could effect how you grade my papers, but I assure you it is from the heart.*" (OK guys, for this one just make up a saucy dream that I had about my instructor who is pretty good looking anyway. Make it romantic and all kind of nasty, but like it all came from my subconscious, so I can't be responsible for what my heart wants. And then if she wants to make the next move, its out there, but its not like I am risking anything cuz I can always plead ignorance and blame my brain.)

REVERSE DREAM ANALYSIS

Dream One

It was a dream in which I walked somewhere in
the desert, when I suddenly saw a silhouette of
my mother. I noticed at once that something was
wrong. I approached to my mother but she turned
away. However, it is her body that turned but her
face remained still and I noticed that she had
three heads. She told me something I could not
hear. I stepped closer but suddenly she rocketed
high into the sky on the balloon. I saw how the
balloons banged high because I lost my consciousness and this dream repeated over and over again.

Dream 2

This dream occurs to me over and over again.
I find myself in a strange forest, where I discover spaceship. When I enter spaceship, I see
strange badgers there. Some wear glasses, others
read books, other badgers make some chemical ex-
periments. In the middle of the ship, I found the
large badger, who is thrice as large. The chef
badger was a judge who solved all the disputes.
Suddenly, spaceship was started to vibrate and I
jumped out of it. When spaceship flew away, I came
closer and saw a human footprint on the ground.

Dream 3

In dream I saw my instructor reading through
the paper I have passed to him. He told me that I
had problems and I grew nervous because I did need
to pass the paper. When he started to tell me
that I have failed, I started to plead as I did it
in my childhood, when my father was angry on me.
I grew more and more nervous suddenly.

RE: reverse dream analysis

Dear Kind Sir or Gentle Madame,

My professor read the dreams you sent me and immediately called the mental authorities. I am writing you from the dreadful confines of *Mushtime Hospital For The Criminally Insane* in Mushtime, Georgia. They told me that my dreams mean that I am a *Class 7 schizopathetic psyssyopath*, so they done the responsible thing and locked me up. When I tried screaming, *"My dreams aren't MINE — they were SENT to me!"* It merely reinforced their confidence in my "delusional headwrongth".

They assured me their diagnosis is rock solid, as it was triple checked by the Dreamputronic Analterpreter 3000. This means that YOU are the one who is MindSnapped©. My beautiful body is suffering the wrath of your brain's disease. I have taken the fall for YOUR crazy, I've taken YOUR nuts to my face.

 I need to convince them of my sanity.

Please. Dream me up a radically normal dream — or else I will be eaten alive by these psychos in here. It isn't safe here. I'm scared. My drooling gorilla of a cell mate has been eyeing my poor head like it's a hot sack of bananas soaked in monkey-nip. This morning he went online and ordered a pack of fruitmatches and a book on how to prepare *'Bananas Foster flambe'*. I might only have 2 to 14 days to live, depending on whether he chose the expedited shipping option on the book. The cost for next-day delivery is usually substantial, so lets pray he has a cheap streak.

I need you to write me a dream so insanely mundane it blows the doctor's face out the back of his cutoff jeans.

Clean up this mess: Write me the blandest dream humanly possible. A dream so dull their beards will drip off their skulls and slide down into the eyes of the secret men that hide in their shoes (I just KNOW it).

Me need a dream that screams "I'M NORRRRMAAAAAL!!!"

<u>Reverse Dream Analysis: New Dream</u>

Recently I have a dream where I was wandering in a house. I knew that it was my house, where I lived with my family. I approached each door and opened it. In the first room, I saw an ordinary kitchen with a dining table, a fridge and some kitchen utensils, but the room was empty and I went on to the next room. When I opened the door of the next room, it was a bedroom, where there was a bed and some furniture. I opened the door of the next room and saw another bedroom, which was probably my parent's bedroom because I saw photos of my parents in the room near the bed.

ASSIGNMENT 29: SUMMARIZE GREAT BOOKS
Reading Comprehension Assignment

Mortals,

I am taking a class called "Books". It would be fun, except for in the classroom there's this jerk who has such a mammoth ego he calls himself "The Professor", and he expects me to read a bunch of things called "books". Even if I wanted to, I can't find any of the so-called books on this list. Please track down each of these alleged books, read each one carefully and summarize the plots of each.

1. How To Break Into Burglary

2. In God We Thrust, In Butts We Nut

3. The Many Minstrel Cycles of Chinkerbell

4. Hello Stigmata, Hello Stigfata

5. Bacchanalia of One Part 2: the Lonely Bacchant is Back…for Revenge!

6. What Evs? These Evs!

7. Perineum Misbehavin'

Thanks!

Vin Chanchre

"How To Break Into Burglary" is a book about what make bur-glars keep on breaking into people's houses and steal. The book talks of how burglars decide them break into houses and steal (Akers & Jensen, 2007).

"In God We Thrust, In Butts We Nut" story is about Christian in United States of America defending their religion against the liberals who are agitating for the removal of religious phrases from money and other public places (Chalker, 2005).

"The Many Minstrel Cycles of Chinkerbell" talks of the ra-cial slur that most people use against others because of the stereotypes that they associate them with, for instance the beggar to refer to African that want things for nothings (Zas-trow & Kirst-Ashman, 2009).

"Hello Stigmata, Hello Stigfata" The book tells of a wound-ed man who is injured and his wounds are too deep to help groom her and another man comes and takes him to hospital. (Leighton & Loori, 2002).

"Bacchanalia Of One Part 2: The Lonely Bacchant Is Back… For Revenge" is a story about Dionysus who was the head of bac-chanalia returning to his birthplace, then exert revenge on Pentheus and women who did not believe Zeus. (Kezich, 07).

"What Evs? These Evs!" Evs is "Ensembles with Variable structure" is an approach through which people interact with flexible structure and diverse elements ensuring compatibility of the elements characteristics (Sulis & Trofimova, 2001)

"Perineum Mishehavin" The area among the anus and the scro-tum in the male and among the anus and the vulva (the labial gap to the vagina) in the female is called the Perineum. This book tells about the problem comes out with this body part and their effects on the malest. (Aklin, 2001)

RE: Order no. 79814AL S

Hey Dudes/ettes!

I hired someone to read over the paper you sent – just to check it for errors, offenses, insults, filthy hidden codes, treason, threats of violence against man or beast, lengthy anti-Semitic diatribes, unnecessarily rambling lists, jam stains, nougat stains, etc. The Checking Service was quite pleased with your work! They only made one suggestion/demand for one (free) revision to the paper before submittal to my professor.

Here it is:

It could be inferred from the unnatural fixation on burglary (in your description of "How To Break Into Burglary") that I myself may be planning on committing such a crime. As if! So, just to cover my hind end of these suspicions (and in light of the recent rash of crime in and around my professor's chalet), it has been suggested that you *"include a clear denial of any intent to burglarize from my professor"*.

It sounds crazy, but just in case, you had better delicately mention in the context of the book description that I would never think about stealing from anyone — even if I had happened to find a spare key to their chalet.

Thanks!!

And may the Lord shine his good spew all on your parts!

(revision)

READING COMPREHEND

    "How To Break Into Burglary" is a book about what make burglars keep on breaking into people's houses and steal. The book talks of how burglars decide to break into houses and steal (Akers & Jensen, 2007). Despite the fact that books, clear outlines the tactics of burglars I would like to emphasize that it has no impact over my characters, as I cannot heed to the information I got from the book. I cannot attempt such delinquent behavior considering that it is unacceptable to the norms of the society. As a rightfully individual I cannot engage in burglaring even having a spare key to a particular room or the home.

ASSIGNMENT 30: GREAT LIT ALT ENDS

Dear TermPaperTown,

My midterm thesis essay paper is an exploration of Alternate Endings To Great Works of Literature. All I need from you is to come up with some Alternate endings to some Great works of literature.

1. Write the ending of _Wizard of Oz_ wherein the Scarecrow and the Tin Man realize they are deeply in gay love with each other.
2. Write an ending to _Gone With The Wind_ where Hitler runs in at the end and saves the day.
3. Provide a new ending to _Catcher In The Rye_ where Holden Caulfield turns into a crawfish and goes into some kind of retail business.

Thanks a bunch... of junk!!

GREAT LITERATURE ALTERNATE ENDINGS

The Wizard of Oz: Chapter 18

The Tin Woodman came in and wept for several minutes, and watched the tears carefully and wiped them away with the towel. When he had finished, the Scarecrow oiled him thoroughly with his jeweled oil-can, to guard against mishap.

"You are so gentle with that," said the Tin Woodsman. "It feels wonderful." Then his heart started to thump very loudly, because you see he had a little girl's heart and he loved the Scarecrow. The Scarecrow said, "you must stay with me. I can keep you oiled and shiny and you can keep me stuffed and protect me from fire."

"Yes," Tin Woodsman agreed. "We make a fine couple."

THE END

Gone with the Wind

So Scarlett went back to Tara and when she arrived there was a group of men camped in the meadow. A funny little man with tiny moustache was leading them and he begged her indulgence. "I am hiding in the past from my enemies.

Scarlett brought towels and warm water and cleaned the cut on his head. When she done she said, "You should really stay the night before you travel. I can give you horse."

"I don't think so, my dear," he said. "I heard what you said, and now I'm of a mind to stay a while, maybe a long while."

She thought, "Well, tomorrow is another day, and we can take it one day at a time."

THE END

Catcher in the Rye

Well this psychoanalysis guy keeps askin' me if I'm goin' back to school. I finally told I couldn't on acounta they don't allow crawdads in school. "No." I says I can't go back to school. I think I'll open a pearl shop. I got these friends make fresh water pearls. They's oysters. An I kin sell them pearls for a lot of money. I don't need no school," says I.

So he says that's ok, shakes his head and tells me to go back to my room. I'm livin' in this here roomin' house, big un it is. Well I'll jus sleep a bit and then go collect some pearls ta sell. I do ok

THE END

ASSIGNMENT 31: PHILOSOPHICAL ALGEBRAICS
Cracking The Existential Equation

Last week my Advanced Mathematics professor came over to the auditorium to watch me wrestle for the first time. Nobody else showed up, so after we broke in, it was just me writhing around on the mat with every piece of sports gear I could find, and him alone in the stands cheering wildly, until I accidentally beaned him right in the beans with a fly ball. He rolled on the ground shrieking in such pain that I had no choice but to step up to the plate and run away as fast as I could and pretend the whole thing never happened.

Well, now my professor claims that as he lay shivering in a widening pool of his own muck, the Grand And Final Equation Of Life Itself materialized and hovered before him. He told me if I solve it, I'll not only get extra credit, but he might do me a favor and stop with the screaming in agony in my ear. Here's the equation - balls in your court:

Given that:

a = Truth
b = God
c = Mother
d = Peanuts
e = Logic
f = Donkey
g = Death

Solve the following formula:

$$\frac{e+b}{a(f-d)+g(c+d)} = n$$

(Solve for n)

Using words, explain in a clear rapturous sentence what (n) means. Then, in another sentence explain what (n) would mean to a mere animal, and how it might change his or her dismal beast of a life.

Vaul Chellow

PHILOSPHICAL ALGEBRAICS SOLUTION

In this equation, n = "religion". The equation uses the following symbolic allegories: Mother is the allegory for human beings, Donkey is the allegory for animals, peanut is the allegorical image for the "core", "kernel" essence of things. Thus, the existential equation described above states that religion is the logical justification of the existence of God which was created by human beings in their fear of death in the attempt to learn and understand the core essence of living, while animals do not possess the fear of death and consequently are not driven to understand the truth and the essence of being, thus intuitively grasping the truth in their lives.

For a mere animal, this mean that the life of animal is not affected by fear of death as it happens with human beings, and animal does not use logic and belief for cognition purpose, it automatically acts in the most truthful way. Thus, animals automatically follow their purpose of being, without having such an instrument as religion.

RE: PaperExcellence #512344 delivery

Hey,

After receiving your solution, I spent 5 hours curled in the fetal position shivering and twittering in anguish. This grew uncomfortable, so I switched positions and wept doggie style for a few hours. Then I thought maybe I was overreacting, since I had not yet read what you wrote. Well, now I *have* read it. And if anything, I underreacted.

I was rocked to the core of my bone at your vicious critique of all religions as "so desperate and lame" as to be "beneath even mere animals". If animals don't have religion, then they are all going to hell! Then it hit me like a sack full of human chins slamming into a thick wall made of pelican tonsils — I need to save the animals! To bring the beasts to Christ!

I immediately dropped out of college to devote my life to spreading the gospel to creature kind, but then it occurred to me that I cannot speak beast. No matter how loudly I scream the good news into their little faces, the critters just look at me like *I'm* the crazy one. And then they try to hurt me — the only person who truly cares about them! I am committed to helping all animals get into heaven, but on the other hand, I can't afford to get any more fingers bitten off. So I built a Veterinary Seminary where animals can teach *each other* how to become Beasts Of The Cloth. All because of you.

If I do this right, I'll be The Jesus to all animals. Then my dad will *have* to admit I'm a special little boy. Or else I'll command my beastly supplicants to tear his neck right out. This was all your idea, so I'd like your help on making it work. Here's what I need you to do: Please write me an essay teaching me a few methods (using treats as rewards?) for making animals (badgers, emus, newts, etc.) as Christian as possible within the limits of the spiritual prison of their "animal-ness".

Thanks!!

Vaul Chellow

VETERINARIAN SEMINARY: SAVING ANIMALS (revision)

Since the time immemorial, Christians have treated animals as an inferior creature. However, animals can give promise of good doing to God, they can pledge their life to Jesus. By leading life according to principles of Christianity. Animal can confess to their sins by admitting that they have done something wrong and will abstain from it in future.

However, animals cannot use their savage brute strength to enforce God's will on humanity as God is the best judge by himself and he can take the righteous decision.

Is there a way to sell holy host dog wafers that make their own gravy in water? No, it would be better to make some kind of holy wet food, which can be eaten by dog easily. Wafers cannot remain holy during the procedures they are manufactured.

Men and animals both have similar origin, both came from one God and thus dogs do not have separate Jesus, they worship the human one.

ASSIGNMENT 32: HOLLYWOOD SCREEN TREATMENT
Cinematic Cash-in

Listen up,

I'm in a pretty tight spot financially right now. So I need you to write an outline for an original Hollywood comedy movie called: "Three Ladies and A Little Goombah Mook". Once I sell it to Hollywood I will be back on my fiscal feet. The basic premise is this:

"Three very proper single ladies are roommates in a distinguished upper class fancy apartment building. One day they find on their doorstep a tiny baby who has the straight-talking, roughneck attitude of a manly Italian goombah mook who speaks in thuggish Brooklynese. The small greasy child's crude and honest manner eventually teaches the proper ladies how to loosen up and enjoy this miserable thing called life."

The outline must track a delightful ROMP of a STORY with outrageous CHARACTERS and must include at least 5 ZANY ADVENTURES, 3 WACKY MISUNDERSTANDINGS, ONE hilarious HIJINK and half a SHENANIGAN. It should make you laugh, make you think, and make me rich.

$$$$$$,

Veilding Chawson

"3 LITTLE LADIES AND A GOOMBAH MOOK"

Three upper-class ladies, who are old friends, stay in the Plazza, where they meet annually since their graduation from the University. Once, they open the door of their suit to find a small, Italian kid from Brooklyn on their doorway asking for help to find his mother. Ladies attempt to teach the thuggish kid but the kid turns out to be teaching them. They stay in Plaza hotel to show the new world to the kid but he just makes fun of everything he sees there. In the hotel, the kid wears slippers and tells a lady "I've got slippiz", while the lady believes the kid is sleepy and attempts to send him to bed. Slippers - slippiz.

As the ladies and the kid goes to Plaza hotel, the kid hears how the ladies call the hotel and starts repeating "I wanna Plee-azza", while a lady, who has just talked on her phone about some legal case, drops distractedly "You're too small to plead" Plaza - Plee-azz-a. The ladies stayed in the Plaza Hotel.

Their suit is on eleventh store. They decided to dine out and took the kid. They descend, take a cab, but the kid tells they left their suit door unlocked. They all get off the cab and come back to find the door pretty locked, while the kid stays at the hall of the hotel and amuses. The kid comes into the room and tells a lady that a police officer asks her downstairs. As the lady walks out, the kid steals her purse.

Ladies and the kid travel down Brooklyn. As the ladies and the kid walks down town, the kid is starting to ask the ladies to pay for a "caw fee", meaning coffee and the ladies cannot understand it believe the kid asks them to pay a caw fee. Coffee - cawfee. When the three ladies and a kid travel throughout New York, the kid tells that they have got a flat tire. As ladies stop the car and go out to look at the flat tire, the kid escapes from them as a shenanigan. Finally, the ladies find the mother of the kid, who turns out to be a friend of theirs, Donna.

ASSIGNMENT 33: CULINARY DELIGHTMAKING
Create A Recipie Using Meconium

Greeting,

I am a frosh/soph/josh/slop at the local corner Culinary Academy. Our big final assignment is a challenge: *"Develop an original recipe whose primary ingredient is meconium"*. I don't know what "meconium" is — or how to cook with it. Please find out and write the definition of meconium, and then write a new recipe for a delicious meal containing mostly meconium as the main ingredient.

Thanks!

And may the Good Lord slop a massive load of his blessings all over your face.

Vender Chenda

A Recipe Using Meconium

Meconium is the thick dark green first stool of newborn human infants. It mainly comprises tissues and cells from intestines, swallowed amitotic fluid, bile secretions, mucus and other enzymes.

Below is a new great way to use summer vegetables with meconium to prepare a delicious stew with high nutrition content.

Ingredients:

1 cup of meconium
2 cups water
1 cube vegetable bouillon, low sodium
2 cups white potatoes cut in 2-inch strips
2 cups carrots, sliced
4 cups summer squash cut in 1-inch squares
1 teaspoon thyme
2 cloves garlic, minced
1 cup onion, coarsely chopped
1 cup tomatoes, diced
2 cups of raw egg

Instructions:

1. Put water and bouillon in a large pot and boil.
2. Add carrots and potatoes and simmer for 6 minutes.
3. Add remaining ingredients, except meconium and tomatoes, then continue cooking for 10 minutes over moderate heat.
4. Remove 3 chunks of squash and puree in blender.
5. Return pureed mixture to pot and let cook for 15 minutes.
6. Add meconium gently and stir for 5 minutes.
7. Remove from heat and let sit for 10 minutes to allow stew to thicken.

Yield: 6 Servings. Serving size: 2 cups. Cal: 120 Fat: 1 g.
Sodium: 196 mg. Protein: 4g. Cholesterol: 0 mg.

ASSIGNMENT 34: ENLIGHTENMENTAL WISDOMS
Answering Koans

Dear PerfectPapersFast,

My Spiritual Guru, Yogi Hamish Bulgur, contends that there are certain questions in the universe that I simply cannot answer. I don't know why he refuses to believe in me. If I wanted to be barraged with insults, I'd seek metaphysical guidance from my mom. And if I can't secure the respect of a man who saunters all over town in just a robe (no jockstrap, scroat *a-swangin*), then whom can I impress? I vow to answer the Yogi's so-called "unanswerable zen koans". That will show him that I'm my own man! At least in his eyes! (The eyes that really count!) Only problem is that I am totally stumped by these intolerably sacred enigmas. But just now I totally realized I could have YOU answer them for me. Pretty clever, right? Who's enlightened NOW?

Please provide clear, concrete answers to the following timeless cosmic conundrums:

1. *What is the sound of one hand clapping?*
2. *If a tree falls in the forest and no one is around to hear it, does it make a sound?*
3. *Does this rash look infected to you?*
4. *Why do they call it a "watch"? I mean, you don't watch it. They should call it a "glance", am I right folks?*
5. *What do tacos dream of?*
6. *How many Hitlers would it take to lift a 1991 Lamborghini Diablo?*
7. *Why is there no answer to this question?*
8. *How does a blind person know when he done wiping my arse?*

Vonti Charles

Answering to the Questions of the Universe

1. What is the sound of one hand clapping?

The sound of one hand clapping is from snapping your fingers.

2. If a tree falls in the forest and no one is around to hear it, does it make a sound?

Yes, but only if the wind is watching.

3. Does this rash look infected to you?

Do not ask if the rash is infected.

4. Why do they call it a "watch"? I mean, you don't watch it. They should call it a "glance", am I right folks?

Don't watch or glance at your timepiece. Lie beneath the stars and watch the heavens unfold.

5. What do tacos dream of?

They dream of sound and color the bright yellows of the sun and the strum of guitars.

6. How many Hitlers would it take to lift a Lamborghini?

It would only take one Hitler, because the universe could not handle more than one Hitler.

7. Why is there no answer to this question?

Need I say more?

8. How does a blind person know when he done wiping my arse?

Take responsibility for your own actions.

ASSIGNMENT 35: PRESS RELEASE FOR SHAME PRIDE PARADE

Hi

There are a lot of pride parades in my neighborhood. But none for me. I want to orchestrate a nice parade for people to get together and celebrate the shame they feel for their own bodies. Please write the press release for the "1st Annual Shame Pride Parade" so I can send it out to the local media. Only people who feel crippling Shame about their human flesh are welcome. Make the press release exciting. Explain the need for such a parade in short sensual, tantalizing sentences! We want to get at least 10 thousand marchers in the parade. And please don't embarrass me. I am quite on edge these days, ever since that weird green thing up and latched onto my sack.

Bye

For Immediate Release:

1st Annual Shame Pride Parade

After extensive consultations with my proxies, I have decided to host the 1st Annual Shame Pride Parade. It is unfortunate to note that most individuals feel ashamed of their body physique.

I wish to bring to the attention of the members of the public that God created human beings in a unique manner. It has come to my notice that the majority of people feel ashamed of their body outlooks. In order to sensitize people notwithstanding, I have convened a Sham Pride Parade scheduled for 1st November, 2012. During this occasion, all individuals who feel crippling shame on their bodies will march into the parade. The activities scheduled for the day, will include talent exhibition with respect to the participation of personalities, who feel ashamed with their bodies in different perspectives.

The judges of the day will assess the talent exhibition competitively to allow rewarding of the best performers. The hosting of the parade will inculcate the essence of outlook and awareness to the members of the public. I wish to notify the members of the public that the issuance of certificates of participation to all members of the public who will attend the auspicious occasion, will sum up the events of the day.

The individuals involved will undergo counseling to ascertain their status.

ASSIGNMENT 36: SLUNK!® BIO-IMAGINEERING

EZ-EssayAcers,

Every common lug on the street knows that *Sea Monkeys*© are fun pets, and that *Lake Donkeys*™ are pure pleasure to pall around with.   For my Bio-Imagineering Class, I have come up with a new genetic hybrid: *Slunks!*®

Slunks!® combine the excitement of a skunk with all the lovability of a slug and all the pizzazz of an exclamation point!   Frankly, *Slunks!*® are better people than most humans in this cursed world! Please list ten (10) fun activities that can be done with a pet *Slunk!*® to the delight of the whole family! Please describe the accurate scientific way that we will combine the Slug and the skunk thru rigorously forced breeding.

Thanks!!

Veendan Chapada

Bio-Imagineering Slunks

Let me introduce a new genetic hybrid that probably may become a pet for your family. This new creature is called a **slunk**. **Slunks** descend from a skunk and a slug bred by force of insemination of a skunk's ovule with gamete of slug male.

Slunks look quite nice as they inherit the best qualities of their parents. First, **slunks** have anal scent glands, which they can use as a defensive weapon on side of the anus. If **slunk** feels good, usually it happens when you stroke this pet, it smells of a fragrance. But when the animal is full of fear, it stinks horribly.

It is also necessary to mention that **slunks** have a rather interesting look and constitution. They have black-and-white fluffy cochlea in which they often hide asleep. When a **slunk** is inside of it one can use it as a pillow. Do not afraid to injure **slunk** as it has strong muscles.

Further, when **slunk** is hidden in its cochlea it may be used as a boll to play games. That is why, your children may be fond of playing with **slunk**; moreover, it really likes to be a part of a game.

Slunks, as their ancestor gastropods, have no legs and move with the help of abdomen. It looks pretty nice when **slunk** chases its potential food with the speed of a cat. **Slunks** can creep on walls and other vertical planes. It is very useful when you have not much space in your apartments. Leave **slunk** hanging on the wall. **Slunks** are funny pets for children. They can inflate balloons of their slime. So they can be involved during parties and games.

Slunks are very playful creatures - as little kittens. So if you want to have a pet for games, **slunk** will be the best one. Let's also mention that **slunks** are very loud creatures. So if you need an alarm system in your house, **slunk** will be of use. Being middle in size and excellent hiders, they will notify you immediately about any intrusion and will stay unnoticed by the criminal.

Finally, there's nothing better for **slunk** than to swim. Its body is designated to be the best swimmer in the world.

ASSIGNMENT 37: SENTENCE FINISHISM 301

"Using at least twenty words, finish this sentence...

SENTENCE FINISHISM

"Finishism" is an advanced word, which describe the superlative degree of finish. It shows the interest to finish the
work on the extreme level.

RE: Finishism ac189099

Dear Sir, or Madam, or....

Unfortunately, you did not correctly complete the assignment that was very specifically etc…

To do it correctly, you need to take the beginning of the sentence that was provided ("Using at least 20 words, finish this sentence…") and bring it to such a satisfying completion that there is… some… stuff… that…

I would do it myself, but I've never been a good at closings or conclusions, because I've always been more of the kind of a guy who sorta… starts strong then… sorta… can't… kind of…

SENTENCE FINISHISM

"Finishism" comes from the finish verb. It shows the superlative degree of completing the work.

RE:RE: Finishism ac189099

Dear Sir or Feminine Person,

You did not correctly complete the assignment so I must request a revision, if you think you are up to it. I would do it myself, but I've been so swamped ever since I declared my major in Reverse Psychology. Then again, maybe you CAN'T do the assignment because it is probably too hard for you. Not everyone is up to the challenge. I guess you just don't have it in you. But if, on the off chance it isn't too much for you, please make sure that you:

1.) FINISH the sentence by ADDING AT LEAST 20 WORDS to what is there.

2.) Make sure that the one and only sentence you give me BEGINS with the words "Using at least 20 words, finish this sentence..."

3.) That is ALL... it is pretty simple for most people, but maybe only really special people can do it... even though it should be easy... but maybe, I guess YOU can't do it because you just aren't good at things... or ARE you???

Good luck and sorry I can't do it myself, but I am so busy on my midterm paper *"Responsibility Shirking In American Letters"* for my class in Advanced Fobbing.

SENTENCE FINISHISM

Teacher said to the students in the Class, using at least twenty words, finish this sentence. This sentence is finish.

RE:RE:RE: Finishism ac189099

Wonderful job!
Stellar work! You ought to be deeply proud of yourself. Now... I don't wish to be a 'Jimmy Sticklerpants'*, but I do have just a few minor criticisms concerning your otherwise breathtaking achievement:

1... You gave me two sentences instead of one, as was requested.
2... You did not add at least twenty words, as was requested.
3... You did not begin with the phrase "Using at least twenty words, finish this sentence", as was requested.

Other than those subtle flaws, I must say I am floored at the articulate grace of your writing. You are a naturally stunning wordsmith. In fact, I am not ashamed to admit that I am embarrassed to reveal that your lyrical couplet brought me to tears thrice. Plus, I am a sucker for twist endings, so you can imagine how low my jaw swung open when I got to the last word. My mouth remains agape to this day, and has become a rather cozy sanctuary for a whole host of egg-laying insects. And the character of 'Teacher' spoke to me in a moving way (perhaps because my own father was a teacher who never spoke to me and moved away.)

I don't want to get ahead of myself, but I have begun to look into the possibility of selling the piece to Hollywood so that it can be adapted into a major motion picture. It feels inevitable. But I want to make absolutely sure that the work isn't cheapened in the process (I see loads of explosions... and that's just the front of my slacks) or watered down (slack backs) or stripped of its 'power on the page'© and turned into 'popcorn pap'© (in fact, that could be a good title for it!).

Anyway, before we get too far into the development process and discussions concerning how many points on the back end I'm going to need to offset the expense of repairing my slacks, I was wondering if you could find a moment to do the assignment correctly?

Thanks!

(* Technically, I could point out that his full name is actually *James Rodelius Sticklerslacks'*, but I don't wanna be a Johnny Specificityhead.)

SENTENCE FINISHISM

"Using at least twenty words, finish this sentence". It was the advice of the teacher to the students in the class.

RE:RE:RE:RE: Finishism ac189099

Naturally,

I reached for a razor the moment I read your re-re-re-redraft, but I managed to tame my hand before it had dug too deeply into my poor throat. This is a major personal breakthrough! Who knew I had such strength? I only wish my dead father could see me now. Unfortunately, even with his lids propped open by toothpicks, he just stares out with eyes so cold, you can practically hear them shrieking "why have you dug me up and forced me to wear this gossamer unitard?"

After your latest sad stab at the sentence, our movie deal has crumbled into so much dust and taffy. At this point I am just hoping that I escape this ordeal alive. With some of that free taffy in mouth!

No pressure, but this assignment is the very last task I need to complete in order to graduate. Also, last week I met the woman of my dreams, but she told me she will not fall in love with me unless I graduate. Additionally, my University is awaiting desperately needed funds to remain open, but they will only receive those funds once the last student graduates — and that last student is the gentleman who is currently wearing the slacks I have on (hint: I wear my own slacks). It also bears mentioning that the university is the financial crux of the county, so if it goes under, the town will be forced to declare bankruptcy, causing hundreds of people to become unemployed. In the best-case scenario, thousands would become homeless.

A state of emergency has been declared. Most of the townsfolk have spent the last few days huddled here in the rec center, preparing for the worst, carefully rationing our food. At meal times, we usually split a can of beans. We have a tiny knife that carves each bean into thirds. Some folks like the center cut of the bean, but I'm an end man myself. We spend our days praying together, swaying hither, fro and yo, whilst chanting. This is our chant:

- USING AT LEAST 20 WORDS, FINISH THIS SENTENCE…
- IT MUST BE ALL ONE SENTENCE, NOT TWO SENTENCES!!!
- YOU MUST ADD AT LEAST TWENTY (20) WORDS!!!
- SO THE TOTAL NUMBER OF WORDS IN THE SENTENCE MUST BE AT LEAST 28!!

Please do the assignment correctly. We're all depending on you.

SENTENCE FINISHISM

Using at least twenty words, finish this sentence was the order by the teacher to his students in the class.

ASSIGNMENT 38: ECONOMICS - CAPITALISM BASICS

Dear My Aids,

I have to write a brief paper explaining what Capitalism is. My Economics professor loves the phrase *"strangle that monkey"*. That is, I assume she *would* like it. I can't say that I have ever heard her use the phrase *"strangle that monkey"*. Or anyone else, come to think of it... But I have a STRONG feeling she thinks that expression is the bee's teats. Please write my essay explaining what Capitalism is, but use the phrase at least 5 times. It's the only way I can think of to really impress her — and I want an A so bad I could choke a pony.

Thanks!

Varsh Charamba

Economics: Capitalism

What Capitalism is?

In the economic system of The Capitalism, the most productive assets are in the custody of private owners instead of strangling that monkey. However, the decision in regards of distribution and production and distribution is taken by the market instead the command of governmental organs. It's like "strangle the monkey", where the only entity has all rights, the Capitalism is suggesting a system minimum involvement or connection of government in economic market issues. However, some Capitalist Economic System is using the supervision of government like strangling that monkey. (Hunt p.3).

Capitalism leads toward corporate or privatization of production and distribution, where the rights of individual and rights of specifically property are being secured, not to strangle the monkey. The term "Laissez Faire Capitalism" is often used by the people for describing the true Capitalist economic system, but this phrase for capitalism is entirely unnecessary or used as strangle the monkey in economic field. (Emigh p.29).

Works Cited

Hunt, Emery K. Lautzenheiser, Mark History of Economic Thought: A Critical Perspective, M.E. Sharpe, 2011, pp.2-8

Emigh, Rebecca J. The Un-development of capitalism: sectors and markets in fifteenth-century Tuscany, Temple University Press, 2008, pp.25-30

RE: 25521

Thanks a lot, guys.

Yesterday at 5 AM, my teacher staggered into a police station soaked from top hat to toe in tears, cradling a dead monkey. She informed the officer on duty that she had been brainwashed into strangling the poor chimp by "my" (your) essay. She claimed that there were subliminal messages in my (your!) essay that made her believe that her pet monkey was a threat to our (my!!) Capitalist society.

Naturally, the proper authorities snuck straight into my dorm room and punched me awake. Then they cuffed me and punched me back to sleep, which worked out well because if I don't get 8 hours I am a wreck. But I am now saddled with a battery of criminal charges: Endangering Capitalism, Subliminal Malfeasance, Imitating An Officer With A Lisp...

I tried telling them it was not my fault, but that it was actually YOUR fault because YOU were the one who secretly buried those dark hidden commands within the words of the essay like a strand of poison bologna delicately interlaced within the meat of a beef hoagie, but the pigs just screamed that they would give me something to *really* pull out of my ass unless I provided PROOF that it wasn't me, but was in fact YOU who done the bad thing to the monkey.

I am so upset and confused, I don't know if I'll ever stop throwing up. I can barely type this eloquent and melodic condemnation of your behavior through these spastic heaves of spew. So, if you care about me as a person, please respond. I have faith you'll do the right thing.

Varsh Charamba

P.S. - There are subliminal messages in this sentence that will make you do what I say or else you will just "happen" to tear your own face off and feed it to a kitty cat.

No Response

ASSIGNMENT 39: CAMPAIGN SPEECH WRITING

Political Problem,

I wanna be Mayor of Vittleton so bad I can taste it in my sister! The only way I can win this election is if I hatch a plan to overcome a wee nuisance facing our sleepy township: Millions of angry scorpions have taken over. Our cozy cobbled streets are a brown scuttling carpet of furious stinging death. Naturally, city leaders have installed a moat filled with boiling blue window cleaner around the town to keep them out. Only problem is that the moat is preventing the local pit viper snakes from entering city limits, but we rely on vipers to feast on the terrible land bats. Until a few years ago, the bats were kept at bay by the roving hordes of feral swamp cats, but once the swamp cats tasted the yummy meat of the wild rabid baboons (who are plentiful round these parts), the swamp cats wouldn't touch bat flesh with a ten-foot swamp cat spoon.

Of course, we tried just putting bat repellent in the scalding scorpion moat, but, as any city planner knows, bat repellent attracts Africanized Demon WASPS, who can be pesky (fatal venom). The citizenry has made it clear that whoever concocts a plan to keep the Afro-Demon WASP population under control will win the mayoral election.

My solution: We cage the entire town in a humongous steel mosquito net every night. Then during the days, each citizen must wear a leech on his neck. And everyone must sign a loyalty oath to City overlords. The netting will prevent the Africans from flying in, and the leeches secrete a painful enzyme that renders human blood unpalatable to WASPS, who will die out in a few generations. The loyalty oath is just good politics.

I need you to lay out both the pros and the plusses of my solution in a rousing sermon directed at whichever voters happen to be in the park when I hop up on that tire pile and preach the speech. Political secret: Heavy use of the words "ya'll" and "Lord" will sway these rubes.

Deal sweetener: the mayor is paid in all the Slug Pudding he can stomach. If you give me moving oral that yields results, I'll split the creamy reward with you.

Vlumpy Custered

<u>POLITICAL SPEECH</u>

All ya'll fine Vittletonians! I have spent the whole of my life among ya'll, knowing that one day I'd take my last breath among ya'll. The Lord knows my heart, as do ya'll.

I am going to tell ya'll how to solve the problems of this town. The crawling stingers with poison, the rat-faced rabid night-squealers, and the hoards of the African demon. Now, they've pestered us all out of our intelligent minds, for they are a blemish on our beautiful Vittleton like having cheese-burgers for lunch on Sundays! Hold your breath and hear me out!

I say if we want to keep crazy bats out of the town, let's cover it with netting during dark! I say to find peace from the demon wasps, we should all keep a leech on our skins, which will render the wasp venom harmless, Hallelujah.

The crazy bats will get tired of trying to get in and will leave us in peace. So will the wasps! Praise the Lord!

Give me the power to lead ya'll to salvation from these vile creatures. Make me your mayor and ya'll be singing our Lord's praises twice on Sundays! May the Lord bless ya'll and our beautiful Vittleton!

ASSIGNMENT 40: CREATIVE POST-MODERN STORYWRITING 1010101

Dear BestHomeworkExperts,

I am taking a course in taking a course in "meta-writing about meta-writing". Of course, we are learning about learning about the benefits of learning the benefits of the tacky post modern gimmick of incessantly insinuating layers of context upon context, as if it is a legitimately creative act and not just a namby-pamby breach on the sandy, sandy beach of intellectual masturbation sans the intellectual sands.

This week my professor taught us about a professor who teaches us about a professor who proves to us that this relentless reframing is more than just a lazy technique that strokes the ego of the faux-clever writer and faux-knowing reader both by reinforcing a mutually assured, self satisfied hyper- awareness of the surface of the form of the act of writing itself without having to risk the grueling task of truly delving into anything essential or grappling with any core reality beyond the signifiers we use as tools to grapple with the tools we use to grapple with tools we use. This lack of *con*tent makes us con*tent*.

Every week we have to write an original story with an additional layer of *meta* added to it each week. But each week I re-curse my inability to recurse. We are in week five and I'm calling you in to do it. Here's what I need you to do: You must compose an original creative story that is a story within a story within a story about a story within a story about a story about a story. It must constantly collapse into itself and directly reference all five levels. Also, write it in the 51st person.

Vonday Chinmuck

RE: CreativeWriting ORDER#4155b

dear customer -   i am one of the writers who is willing to take care of your order. i am a writer often
write short stories. however before i can request for
the order i would like you to make clear as to how many
levels you want in the story-4 or 5. also do tell me
whether you really meant that the story should be written in the 51st person or was it a typing error and you
meant that it be written in the 1st person?

RE:RE: CreativeWriting ORDER#4155b

Dear Sirs or/and Madame,

I received your short story and I'm ashamed to say that I didn't get it... AT FIRST! On my initial reading I thought you were legitimately asking questions about "levels of meta", but then it occurred to me what a brilliantly reflexive tale you've woven in such a brief passage — incorporating our entire situation of "orchestrating narrative" itself into the narrative! Top flight experimental po-mo fun-fic gents! Whale of a tale! And I love the character of the "writer who is willing to take care" of my order. My eyes misted up at the cleverness of it all, and a hot burst of saliva flushed out under my tongue... and now it won't stop. My mouth is gushing like a dang ol' faucet on full blast. I must've lost half my body water and it shows no sign of letting up.   I'm pruning like a raisin here. (yum!)

And the best part is that your story is a living, growing literary beast! I mean, even these words in this very missive are now part of the tale you've spun! And this word! Also... THIS word (squids). The bad news is that even though I happily admit your piece is a powerful – and... I'm going to say... important – read, I don't think my professor will get it, because she's Danish. And if she somehow does get it, she may become violently enraged with petty bitter jealousy, because she is Danish. Also, I counted, and technically there are 7 levels in your story. Can you redo it but this time make it just 5 levels?

I am sorry if there was any confusion, but my professor is Danish so things can get as discombobulated as a cardamom meatball in a Doberman's snooch. It should be written in the 51st person.

Spoiler alert: I can't wait to look at your next whale tale!

V.V.C.C.

RE:RE:RE: CreativeWriting ORDER#4155b

Dear Student,

i shall try to work on the story. but kindly clarify
your message to me which reads "Re:Re:CreativeWriting
ORDER#4155b". the said message states that i have
submitted some story already and that it is in 7 levels.
however, as i have not yet started work on the order, i
have to admit that i have not submitted any such work
and am unable to understand what that message reads.
kindly clarify.

RE:RE:RE:RE: CreativeWriting ORDER#4155b

Dear Sir Madame, Jr:

Allow me to answer your latest trippy whale of a story within a story within a story (ad infinitum, practically) with my own story within a story without that story within a different, more biting tail:

On a trip to Wales late last sentence, I met a dog named "MetAdog" at the local kilogram (I believe you Americans call them "pounds") and adopted him to suit my kneads. Well... I am devastated to retort that when I opened your most recent e-mail and read this new story (clever/level-y titled "Re:Re:Re:CreativeWriting ORDER#4155b") about this strange protagonist who searches in vain for "kindly clarification", the poor pooch was crushed to death under your multiple layers of narrative! Pull back gents, pull back! The results of your reflexivity reflects on you. Donations in MetAdog's honor can be made to themselves from themselves by themselves about themselves.

V.V.V.C.C.C.

Waiting for Sam and Gene
(A short story in 52 actions)

Ponderously, the mirror entered, supported by others, and others still, followed by others, their glimmer now faint.
'You are not a mirror, are you?'
'Who me? Mirror? My name is Hamm.'
'Pull the other one.'
'That was the other side of the story. There's always the other side of the story. This side, we're in the mirror, and Nagg there slides. Sorry - cracks.'
'That's not Nagg. It's a woman, and besides, it's Nagg's reflection. Nagg went through the looking glass like Alice.'
'Alice! Now here you go, mixing up hash and mash.'
'And trash, and bash.'
She turned to the other two, or their reflections: she did not distinguish, not wanting to be taken for a sexist, ageist, racist or reflectionist. 'Again!? Do you mean the kind of enlightenment that comes with light, or glory?'
'They are both reflected, dumb-dumb, so either will do.'
'When looking for faults use a mirror, not a telescope.'
A thought-bubble appeared over the 51st action. 'Do I have to say it twice? Some eat apples, some eat mice.'
The others, and the others behind them, released the mirror and it crashed to the floor.
'Now you've done it.'
'Indeed I have. There go twelve years of reflection. Shards, pretty shards.'
'Reflected irony. Never mind seven years of bad luck.'
'Y'know, these days, magnification's the thing.'
They all sighed. Condensation fogged them all. 'Stop her, someone. She's starting again.'
'Again!?!' They all shrieked.
'Do I have to say it...?'
'Hush,' said the mirror at the wall. Here come Samuel and Eugene.'
'What - do we all do it all, all over again? All?'
'All what, idiot?'
They all pulled purple screens over their surfaces. It went suddenly dark. Or light.

Waiting for Sam and Gene
(A short story in 52 actions)

Ponderously, the mirror entered, supported by others, and oth-
ers still, followed by others, their glimmer now faint.
  'You are not a mirror, are you?'
  'Who me? Mirror? My name is Hamm.'
  'Pull the other one.'
  'That was the other side of the story. There's always the
other side of the story. This side, we're in the mirror, and
Nagg there slides. Sorry - cracks.'
  'That's not Nagg. It's a woman, and besides, it's Nagg's re-
flection. Nagg went through the looking glass like Alice.'
  'Alice! Now here you go, mixing up bash and mash.'
  'And trash, and bash.'
  She turned to the other two, or their reflections: she did
not distinguish, not wanting to be taken for a sexist, age-
ist, racist or reflectionist. 'Again!? Do you mean the kind of
enlightenment that comes with light, or glory?'
  'They are both reflected, dumb-dumb, so either will do.'
  'When looking for faults use a mirror, not a telescope.'
  A thought-bubble appeared over the 51st action. 'Do I have to
say it twice? Some eat apples, some eat mice.'
  The others, and the others behind them, released the mirror
and it crashed to the floor.
  'Now you've done it.'
  'Indeed I have. There go twelve years of reflection. Shards,
pretty shards.'
  'Reflected irony. Never mind seven years of bad luck.'
  'Y'know, these days, magnification's the thing.'
  They all sighed. Condensation fogged them all. 'Stop her,
someone. She's starting again.'
  'Again!?' They all shrieked.
  'Do I have to say it...?'
  'Hush,' said the mirror at the wall. Here come Samuel and Eu-
gene.'
  'What - do we all do it all, all over again? All?'
  'All what, idiot?'
  They all pulled purple screens over their surfaces. It went
suddenly dark. Or light.

ASSIGNMENT 41: BAD BUSINESS IDEAS

To Whom This Is Addressed:

Sometimes (fact: often) a businessman must chose to do the morally repugnant thing — it's just good business! One mustn't be hemmed in by Dame Decency, that lusty whore. So, in order to stretch our "capacity for hideous behavoir" muscles and get our consciences nice and numb, our class is training to fabricate some top-shelf wrongh.

Thusfore, my Business Professor has given us an assignment to invent the worst business ideas imaginable in the following fields:

1. A really fun toy for kids that is so dangerous it would likely kill them.
2. A product for drivers that is too racially offensive to be successful.
3. Something that every church should have, but that would also destroy the faith of the churchgoers.

For each of these 3 products, you must answer just 4 questions.

1. What is the name of the terrible product?
2. What does it do?
3. Why is it terrible?
4. What is a really clever promotional slogan for it?

Vercnan Chanmat

Bad Business Ideas

1. **VirtuaAction** is a toy for children that lets them play in a virtual environment using real props. For example they can wrestle with each other using a real person as a competitor while the game creates a simulation. It's such a terrible product for children because if they fight while thinking they are in a real like environment they could injure themselves or the other player critically. Its promotional slogan is: "Fun only seems real!"

2. **Slavegrance** is a car air freshener that is shaped like an African American slave from the old times. One model is in the shape of a black male that is holding a pitch fork, and the fragrance comes out of the pitch fork. It's a very racially offensive product because it depicts a time when African Americans were treated very badly and in an inhumane manner. The slogan for this product is: "Keeps your car refreshed like your own personal slave."

3. **SoulFood** is the evil album that is being sold by a group of churches to raise much needed funds. It is such a bad idea because many people turn towards religion to get away from the materialistic ideas and when they would see a church doing this they might get skeptical. This could lead to deep mistrust towards the church. The slogan for this product is: "Money vibes that lift your spirit!"

ASSIGNMENT 42: LINGUISTICS 102
Linguistic Limits (Invent A New Language To Overcome Them)

Sup. I don't know where to even start with this assinment... it's so dumn and it's like... I'd rather remov my prized raisin collektshun frum my mouf (no way!) than right this stupid essay... so you guys just do it for me. Here're the assinment:

Human language cannot encapsulate the swirling subtleties or ethereal complexities of human thought and emotion. Write an essay explaining the fundamental failure of ALL languages invented by mankind and then correct this problem for the good of humanity.

- Part one of the essay should be a lyrical lament on the woeful deficiencies of language herself. One by one, it must accuse every single word in history of being a cruel mockery of the notion it is meant to evoke. It must convince the reader that so-called "words" are not fit to lick the skeet-flecked feculence off of the bloodstained jackboots of Actuality. In a nutshell — it should make one yearn to frantically pound one's ham-like man-fists against all signifiers — the sick shell of that very nut.

- Part two of the essay is to be written in an entirely NEW language invented by the writer with no connection to any language of earth. In this new language, you are to express a thought or feeling that has heretofore never been able to be put into words by man or beast. This message is to be crystalline in its clarity, razor-like in its accuracy and soul shittingly poignant.

- Part three should translate perfectly what was expressed in the previous part of the essay, and give some clue as to the breadth and depth AND gredth of what was stated in that new language.

The essay must revolutionize the way mankind communicates, and change the very shape of man's soul, heralding the dawn of a shining new chapter in human history. And for fuck's sake, keep it clean.

Verming Chompman

Linguistic Limits

Stage One

Life has many faces. In the course of history the birth of different races came along. Man communicates with the use of an element: language. In the beginning somewhere in history "And the whole earth was of one language, and of one speech." (Gen 11:1)
    The birth of human language only brought division
    With the aim at confusing all humanity (Gen 11:7)
    Language is now a disease to all.

Stage Two

Hurx adix harawax anax kax banbanchix akwax kurakurx yax atax duniyanix ashinax. Yax kax damuwax a'rx fakux shanx atax kurakurx yax nax adix nax girax wax. Yax kax surx harax shanx ngax yax tax latux kax kurakux dukux.

Stage Three

Life is incomplete with the diverse langauges accros the world today. We have tribal problems, land battles and all due to the confusion brought by language formation. To sovle this problem we need unity

Reference:

The Bible (Denotes King James Version)

RE: ORDER 42666

Well, Well, Well…

When my professor read that essay she got agassed and assed me to stay after class to discus on it. She was very concerned with the language that "I" (you) "invented" (plagiarized!). Yep — the jig is up. She informed me that the language I (you) used in the second stage was NOT made up, but STOLEN from an impoverished and dwindling indigenous tribe native to the tiny underground Jigupian island of Old Guinea Pigeon. She showed me some real sad snaps of the ravaged primitives — they are not cute, and between you and me, barely got me hard. How dare you snatch their precious tongue? My Professor called me "the worst sort of linguistic imperialist pig dog scum sucker, not fit to scrape the cake caked cake from a cake." (I'm not sure I got that quote right — she might of just been stuttering at the end there. She pissed.)

To make matters worse, she found so many typos and grammatical errors in the paragraph, that the language was nearly unrecognizable to her! She says if I (you) don't bring that section up to syntactical snuff she's going to ship me (me!) off to live with the tribe to spend a year washing the cake off their feet. Bumdog Scrillionaire! I can NOT live there! I looked it up and they don't even have beef chalupas!

Please master that forgotten language and make Stage 2 grammatically immaculate, chop-freaking-chop!

Thanks.

P.S. My professor also said that the translation wasn't precisely what "I" had claimed in my paper, but in fact more accurately translates as: *"Once there was a man whose prison was a chair / The man had a monkey, they made the strangest pair / The monkey ruled the man, it climbed inside his head / Now as fate would have it, one of them is dead!"* This of course is the tagline for "Monkey Shines". She claims it is common knowledge that Monkey Shines is one of 3 movies the tribe has ever seen, and that they found it "trite, predictable, and obviously the work of 7 hobgoblins".

Linguistic Limits Corrected

Hurx adix harawax anax kax banbanchix akwax kurakurx yax
atax duniyanix ashinax. Yax kax damuwax a'rx fakux shanx atax
kurakurx yax nax a'dix nax girax wax… Yax kax surx harax shanx
ngax yax tax, latux kax kurakux dukux.

Reference:

The Bible (Denotes King James Version)

ASSIGNMENT 43: CRIMINAL PSYCHOLOGY 120

My assignment is to interview and investigate the Criminal Mind to illuminate the psychological root causes for crime in our society. I managed to get access to and psychologically probe a man who was incarcerated for armed robbery, and I am supposed to write a peircing evaluation of the insights he provided me. Cover:

1. How was the criminal coping with the meat of his haunting guilt?

2. What demons were unleashed during your meaty consultation with the criminal mastermind?

3. How did you get underneath the surface and get at the meat of his pathology?

4. What signs of regret did the subject exhibit? Meat?

5. What techniques did you employ to get the criminal to open up and share the meat of his feelings?

TRANSCRIPT OF ENCOUNTER

Q: First of all I want to thank you for allowing me to visit you in prison for this encounter session.

A: Hey is this a tape recorder? Am I going to be on the radio?

Q: No, this is for a school assignment. I want you to take a moment and tell me, when you meditate on your actions, why do you think you robbed that tire store?

A: I was tired! [subject laughs] Just kidding! I guess it was because… I wanted a wheel of a deal!

Q: Its OK, just… you can talk to me, I won't judge you. Tell me, what makes you feel you had to resort to this crime?

A: I wanted to say "Hands up, this is a rubbery!" [laughs, raises hand for hi five] Up top! I guess I'm on a ROLL now huh? Cuz of the tires?

TRANSCRIPT OF ENCOUNTER (cont'd)

Q: You are making me frustrated, because the point of this encounter is —

A: Ummm… quite the a-TRACTION?

Q: Can we talk sincerely for a moment?

A: Lets see… there's got to be another one… Skid marks! [laughs]

Q: I really need to get some answers for my class assignment.

A: It's a good thing I didn't rob a hat store. That would be a HAT-tastrophy!

Q: I can only help you if you cooperate.

A: Sorry, do I have a bad HAT-tiude? Oh, shit that's the capper!

Q: Oooh I hate you. [whispers to nearby corrections officer, discreetly slips him cash] I've just bribed a guard to do my dark bidding.

A: Aw, why you putting a LID on my fun… No! Officer, back away! Please! [a shadow slithers across his face] Noooooo! [he is no more.]

Psych0-analyze a Real criminal

1.) H0w was the criminal c0ping with the meat of his haunting guilt?

   Criminal is haunted n0t by guilt but by anxiety. He seeks n0t t0 inflict certainties 0n 0thers but t0 find a meaning in life. Liberated fr0m the superstiti0ns 0f the past, he d0ubts even the reality 0f his 0wn existence. His sexual attitudes are permissive rather than puritanical, even th0ugh his eman- cipati0n fr0m ancient tab00s brings him n0 sexual peace.

2.) What dem0ns were unleashed during y0ur meaty c0nsultati0n with the criminal mastermind?

   Dem0ns were unleashed during c0nsultati0n because m0st pe0ple I kn0w are unhappy being label as criminal masterminds 0r speed dem0ns.

3.) H0w did y0u get underneath the surface and get at the meat 0f his path0l0gy?

   My experience 0f 0bserving and helping with criminal was very interesting. This was part 0f and externship that I was d0ing in path0l0gy.

4.) What signs of regret did the subject exhibit? Meat?
    None.

5.) What techniques did y0u empl0y t0 get the criminal t0 0pen up and share the meat of his feelings?

Em0ti0nal risk-taking. T0 have true intimacy with criminals, a pers0n must 0pen up share pers0nal feelings with criminal, is risky because criminal may n0t feel the same way. But it is n0t p0ssible t0 be really cl0se with criminal with0ut being h0nest and 0pen with he/him.

ASSIGNMENT 44: EARLY CHILDHOOD ED 340
Breaking Truths

EZ-Essays,

I done decided to become one of them-there school-teachers, cuz I hear them gets free lunches (file under: yum) and summer off (file under: groove back). But my roomates down at the dump told me I gotsta climb outta the fridge and go to colledge to be a teacher. So I emrolled... and I been attending that-there Princeton University fer bout 3 years now. Here go this here thing that the teacher there is makin me do, the rat:

The greatest challenge to teaching in a public school comes the day you have to break the awful terrifying news about our world to the poor innocent children, who never done nothin' to nobody (no how). Your assignment is to devise several ways to inform young students (so their parents don't have to) about the most horrible realities of existence in a way that makes them not whine and cry and put what a chiropractor could describe as a "crimp" in your day. The goal is to crush their souls so gently, the kids actually kind of like it. Find pleasurable, non-upsetting ways to relay the following to a child aged 4 to 6:

1.) There is no God.
2.) There is no such thing as a soul — once you die you end, and you will definitely die, and be eaten by worms.
3.) Life gets worse with every passing second. (make this seem like a silly, fun game)
4.) I find you physically repugnant and your mommy finds you tiresome.
5.) It is very difficult to open those plastic packages of batteries, am I right?

There's only one rule of the assignment: 1.) Be direct and be blunt. 2.) Make the crushing misery of existence sound great, like a crazy fun party. And 3.) Don't sugar coat anything.

Voorst Chichner

Early Childhood Ed: Breaking Truths

Many issues children take for granted may be different
in the real world. For instance, there is no God and soul.
These issues may be presented to children gently in a pleasurable game.

First, it is necessary to persuade children that God does
not exist. For this purpose, I would suggest them to play
a game, where they should construct their own world. They
should create their own world, with its own inhabitants, such
as animals. They create them and they can do anything they
like with them. As children do all that, I would tell them
that they are just playing God and any person can do exactly
the same thing with creatures. There is always human mind behind any creation and there is no God.

Another game would show children that soul does not exist,
as your life ends, there will be no afterlife. For this purpose, I would suggest children to take a glass of warm water
and a tea spoon of sugar. I would tell that any human being
as well as any being at all is like that sugar. Then I would
suggest them to put the sugar into the warm water that means
that any human disappears as he/she dies just like the sugar
in the warm water. So children would understand that they can
disappear just like the sugar in the warm water. After that I
would suggest them to drink the water and taste how pleasant
it is to make them understand that there is nothing wrong.

ASSIGNMENT 45: JOURNALISM: ADVICE COLUMN

Dear SameDayHomework,

I work at the school newspaper "Duh Fold" at Stanfold University. I write the advice column "Ask Duh AdviceGod". Mostly I answer simple questions like "which babe should I bop?" or "which body could I slop?", but as of late a problem has arisen and it refuses to afall. As you know, there are several gorillas in our university Science Department that have been taught sign language. I have received several letters from these gorillas who have posed questions. I am stumped, I don't know how to respond. Here are the gorilla queries you need to answer for me:

1. Dear AdviceGod: Me like apple. You give me apple? Please yes give apple me yes? Kindly appy me. Sincerely, Appleless and Crabby.

2. Dear AdviceGod: This is a question for a friend of mine, not me. A friend (who isn't me) has been experiencing a burning sensation when I urinate. I mean when HE urinates. My friend wants to know if there is a fire inside his body, or if this is normal. Signed, A Good Friend Of Mine Who Isn't Me, No Way, That's A Ridiculous Accusation

3. Ciao AdviceGod: Me have-a the question. You answer the question? Atsa what-a you do, no? Here go my-a question: If God is good, why does he allow so much suffering in the universe? Is it because of that thing I did in the shower with-a the spicy meatball? Signed-a, Nonymous.

4. Dear AdviceGod: I need your help! I had "relations" with a "real doll" and now I got imitation crabs. Should I boil and eat or kiss and feed them? Love, Love Is A Lie

5. Dear AdviceGod: I know I am just a lowly beast of the field, and this may just be the beef jerky talking, but I think I just saw some talking beef jerky. Please Explain.

The apes quake with the need to knowlege!!

Vera Chomong

JOURNALISM: ADVICE COLUMN

1. Dear Appleless and Crabby: I will bring you an apple some day and we will communicate more. Apples are great for the health and it is important to eat them. Have fun!

2. Dear A Good Friend Of Mine Who Isn't Me: I can say that it is normal and this will pass soon. When you stop paying a lot of attention to it, it will pass sooner! Be careful and be good!

3. Dear Nonymous: It is rather hard to answer this question, but I will try. Some people suffer because they have done something wrong and their conscience does not allow them to relax. Some people are guilty of what they have done.

4. Dear Love Is A Lie: I can advice you to find a new girlfriend and to have more friends to communicate with. Relationships in life are important and almost vital. They are indispensable part of life. Take care of your health and good luck to you!!

5. Dear Please Explain: When there are tough days and imagination works great, it is sometimes possible to see the talking beef jerky. Although you should not pay a lot attention to it and this will pass soon, I tell you! Keep going strong!

ASSIGNMENT 46: ADVERTISING / MARKETING STRATAGEMS

Dear ClassworkRelief,

Study these product descriptions then develop a *mrktg/advzg (marketing and advertising) strat (strategy) for ech'n (each one).* Note these are actual products that have yet to be unveiled. How can we insure our price point is the pointiest? How can we penetrate each consumer deepiest? Best ideas will be passed on to the relevant companies.

<u>Crimcor LUX Trauma Blankets</u> For people who have just been through a horrific trauma such as a car accident or a rape, and they have been wrapped in a blanket by the emergency services workers. The Crimcor LUX Trauma Blanket is a more luxurious, comforting alternative model (that costs just a few hundred dollars extra). Made from a plush blend of deer fur and human hair, and inner-lined with a nice hot casserole for snacking on and showing off. (Target market: traumatized sophisticates, disoriented victims vulnerable to making poor decisions, catastrophiles.)

<u>Strawchos</u> The first full plate of nachos you can *drink*. This is NOT achieved via liquefying nachos, but instead by miniaturizing several plates of nachos and digitally emboldening the straw, so that it can suck up to 800 pounds of pressure per square mouth-inch. (Target market: unfortunate children, lost causes, sad sacks, suckers, sack suckers, folks who want to accidentally choke to death on nachos.)

<u>Maniacal Man Hand Cream</u> This is for the scaly, ultra rich financial baron who is constantly rubbing his wrinkled hands together in gleeful anticipation of exploiting his powerless prey. This sulfur based lotion prevents the delicate the hands of any Machiavellian power denizen from getting too dry, flaky or irritated during his marathon wicked, mouth-watering hand wringing sessions (target market: vile billionaires, dark-hearted trillionaires who profit off of choking hazards).

Create a masterful marketing plan and slogan for each product.

Vather Chom

ADVERTISING/ MARKETING STRATAGEMS

1) **Crimcor LUX Trauma Blanket** - to be marketed to up market clients who become trauma victims. The target market can be reached at the point of need as in high end private hospitals. The product can also be promoted along with premium insurance policies for which most of the rich clients subscribe to. This product should be marketed with the use of personal selling techniques in ambulances.

Proposed slogan: **Crimeco LUX Trauma Blanket - "A cocoon of warmth when you truly need it."**

2) **Strawchos** - The first plate of nachos that can get drunk. The target market consists of kids and kids at heart and parents of kids. The adult will not have much concern for the calorie aspect of the product. The product marketing can make use of special promotions in malls near fast food locations and sports and pop rock arenas in USA.

The proposed slogan: **Strawchos - "Have a sip of Nachos!"**

3) **Maniacal Man Hand Cream** - This product can be marketed via exclusive perfumeries, spas, and health clubs which are frequented by the target clients who are the super rich, middle aged billionaires. The product should be marketed as an essential for hand care and positioned as a highly exclusive product to appeal to the nature of the target group. Some glossy magazine advertisements can be also added to the advertising portfolio.

Proposed slogan: **M&M Hand Cream "for hands worth shaking"**

ASSIGNMENT 47: SPIRITUAL RICHNESS OF HOLISTIC HEALING

So,

A Judge has ordered me to take a course on "Spiritual Centeredness" at the "Holistic Healing N' Halfpriced Hoagies" stand down the street from my mansion. His Honor said if I didn't pass the class like gas, I'd serve 6 months for the "crime" I done. The "crime" was no big whoop: I was minding my own business, just trying to milk myself to death at the Happy Slipper, a bar down the street from my mansion, when the guy on the stool next to me suddenly stood up and claimed that he had once had sensual innercourse with my mama. I leapt to my feet and knocked him out with a 10 lb sack of frozen gravy that I happened to have on my person (don't ask) before I realized it was my own father who'd made the claim. That's when I really started pounding him (ask). I then carved my name in his forehead, sliced my social security number on his neck and wrote my favorite color on his jacket, before I made my getaway. Somehow the cops tracked me down.

Judge thinks I am a "spiritually hollow danger to the world". Truth be told — ain't *that* the truth! I am filled with violent intentions 24-7 (not coincidentally, these are also Denny's hours). I am telling you straight out that this is a desperate cry for help: *Please please help* me write a paper saying I am normal and healthy. Unfortunately, I can't write it because of my burning ache to wreak havoc evermore. This world is a vapid sucking blackness (no offense intended — some of my best friends suck blackness) but I don't wanna go back to prison. The paper must:

1.) Describe how emotionally healthy I am and how I would never resort to yummy extreme paingasmic violence. Mention some specific savage acts I would never even conceive of committing.
2.) List some exceptions where violence is not only acceptable, but glorious.
3.) Please don't mention the voices in my head that order me to kill.
4.) Convince the judge that I am too good (and scary) for prison.
5.) Mention how thankful I am to the Great and Honorable Judge (a little bit o' suck-butt now can avoid a butt load of non-con sensual butt suck in the big house).

Thanks!!

Holistic Healing: Spiritual Richness

The path to spiritual wellness is one full of ups and downs.
Since the day I started doing this course, I have experienced
transformation and peace of mind. The bad things I have ever
thought of like kill anyone who dared disturb me, assault
whores, rob the city bank, burn my neighbor's house, commit
suicide, hurt someone's feelings because everyone is useless,
and others that cannot be mentioned, are no longer part of
me. I now find life worthy and wonderful.

Abusing and insulting anyone who is close to me is not acceptable and I cannot tolerate that. My father abused my
mother in front of all the people in the bar and that was
bad. Such a person is not worth living. It is not acceptable to beat him but in such a situation it will be so. As
much as I was defending my mother, I hate going to prison. I
have changed and I will never do any harm to anyone.

Life in prison is like hell. I hear people die of cholera.
Some nasty things like homosexuality without protection happen there, I hate this and I don't want to be infected with
the bad disease. Cockroach meal is served there and sleep
turns into nightmare. I do not want to die, I am trans-
formed.

Thanks a million times Honorable Judge for been so thoughtful about my life. I am a new person looking forward to gain
eternal life.

RE: ORDER 19131V

Friendo,

I thank you... and the head voices thank you!

The Judge loved your essay. He grabbed my arm and screamed, "every graceful word soared off the page to give elegant voice to my own inarticulate misery." Then he roughly buried his face in my breast to growl, "I was lifted on the wings of your words". (I think he is going through some heavy emotional gunk in his life... perhaps it could be that a certain mysterious sicko has been discreetly pleasing his wife and pets). But then he said, "Your paper is missing only two things, which you must write yourself and not hire some amoral cretins to write for you". So here's what I need you to do once my check clears:

1.) A description of how my father is a useless worm whose black heart should be eaten like an apple by other, more worthy worms.

2.) Write a sentence where I apologize specifically to Jesus's hands for what I have done. The sentence must be addressed to His holy hands and must express heartfelt contrition to those poor palms.

Judge said if I include these two brief elements that I would be released and all charges dropped. Please do a good job on this. I really don't want to be put in the electric chair. It looks like it would be murder on my back.

New Holistic Healing: Spiritual Richness

1.) A description of how my father is a useless worm who's black heart should be eaten like an apple by other, more worthy worms.

My father have always been a source of disharmony. I may blame him also for the way he brought me up as a person without morals, in ignorance of God. Such a person is not worth living.

2.) It must have a sentence in it where I apologize specifically to Jesus's hands for what I have done.

Now my Prayer to God: I pray to you oh God through Jesus Christ; Forgive me for all my sins and transform my life completely, let me be fully and truly yours. I do not take your suffering on earth Jesus for granted anymore. I am so sorry about your hands. Save me Jesus. Thank you Jesus. Amen.

ASSIGNMENT 48: RAISE MY ELEGANCY

MidtermRelief -

My teacher say to me: "you got no elegancy!" She say, "you make me go sick in me pants!" So... you write me an essay that when I read it, I immediately become more suave, elegantic, gracefull, AND dignity.

THANKS BRO!!!

Tips for Improving Elegance Level

In the current era, people are praised a lot for being elegant, and the ones not being so are criticized publicly. Elegance has become a vital component for one's personality to improve their personality.

Various specific tips can be given to improve the elegance level. One should stand straight and sit with crossed legs with folded arms. Positive thinking would bring out good impressions on face and add to the elegance. The clothes an elegant person wears are always clean and ironed in accordance with the occasion.

Another main aspect on which a person is judged is an elegant person always emphasizes on positive things in a positive manner and with clearly pronouncing the words. Use of emotions is only particular when communicating with your best friends and family. For elegance, one should not engage in praising oneself as it is a symbol of foolishness.

The elegant person is also identified by the things he or she buys that actually attracts others rather than annoying their eyes.

RE: RAISE MY ELEGANCY

Ddddrrr Ssssrrr,

It diffficult to tttype thiis with ccrrossed arrmms andd leggs. Also I burrrnned mmmy wwwhole torrso ironnninggg myy shhirrrt — Bbut I havve bbbecome tthe mossst eleggannt mmmann onn eearfff!!!   It tookk a bbuncha exxttra hours to walkk to classs with mmy arrms and legggs folded the wwhole timme. Buttt at Illeast whennn I finallly arrrived, myy tteacher was fffurious att mme.   Sshe calleddd mme "tardy". Not cooool. I havvve a brrrother wwho is mmmental tardyyy.

I haavvve 3 Quessstionns:

1. Whennn cannn I unfffold mmy legggs? (Itss beenn 4444 ddays. The Illeft one is turrning bbblue — wwith elegggggannnce.)

2. Cannn I takke offf mmmy shirrrt bbbeffforre I ironnn it nexxxttt ttime?

3. Whattt shoulddd I ddo wwith all ttthe emotionnsss ttthat I havve helddd innn? (they arrre backkked up ppprretty harrrdd frommm bbbeing helddd dddown, andd I bbbbeen cryyyyinggg forrr 3 ddays stttraighttt. I sstapeleddd my tear dducts ssshut, bbbbut mmmy eyes are severe ppaain abboutt to bblow)

THANKS BRO!!!

Answers For Improving Elegance

1. Whennn cannn I unfffold mmy legggs? (Itss beenn 4444
ddays. The llleft one is turrning bbblue — wwith eleggggg-
gannnce.)

In elegance, it is only required to cross the arms and legs
while in a seated position.

2. Cannn I takke offf mmmy shirrrt bbbeffforre I ironnn it
nexxxttt ttime?

Always remove garments prior to ironing the shirt.

3. Whattt shoulddd I ddo wwith all ttthe emotionnsss ttthat
I havve helddd innn? (they arrre backkked up pppprretty
harrrdd frommm bbbeing helddd dddown, andd I bbbbeen
cryyyyinggg forrr 3 ddays stttraightttt. I sstapeleddd
my tear dducts ssshut, bbbbut mmmy eyes are severe ppaain
abboutt to bblow)

In use of emotions for elegance one must avoid abusing and
use a soft tone for communication with clearly pronouncing
the words.

ASSIGNMENT 49: CAMPAIGN SLOGANS

Dearest Ya'll,

Unless you been livin under a rock, you musta heard by now that I am runnin' for mayor of Vittleton. Well, unfortunately, due to a recent economic downturn, most Vittletonians are forced to live under rocks. But I have been walking through each neighborhood, knocking on rocks and telling voters that I is just like them, even though one time I DID use toilet paper. I explain that I was young, and I was just experimenting. Besides, I only inhaled, I didn't swallow.

One niggling hitch galls and gnaws at the nads of my nuggets — low they swing in their bearded wrinkly sack, crashing smartly against my thighs as I pace in naked angst — I need five campaign slogans to put this thing in the bag!

1. A super catchy way to say that "wearing several leeches on your neck is a splendid way to live as the Lord would've wanted, had he survived his murder."
2. A clever slogan that compares my political acumen favorably to various flavored meats.
3. I thought of a good rhyme but I can't think of the slogan for it. The rhyme is to rhyme my name "Vlumpy Custered" with the phrase "Blusty Pumps". So come up with a kick-tushy slogan that makes that rhyme.
4. A lot of folks love eggs in Vittleton, but most can't afford the yolk or the white of the egg. They can only afford that little white stringy thing that floats inside the egg that is called the chalaza. Make me a slogan that mentions "chalaza."
5. A slogan to appeal to ladies, something that will make even the most female women in town cream they political jeans. In fact, make sure it includes the phrase "jean cream" in it.

These slogans must rival the Great Political Mottos of our time such as Barack Hussein Obarma's "Yes We Could've!" Ike Eisenhower's "Put Some Ike Sauce On It!" and Parven Limindolo's "Shove It On In!"

Vlumpy Custered

POLITICAL CAMPAIGN SLOGANS

1. A super catchy way to say that "wearing several leeches on your neck is a splendid way to live as the Lord would've wanted, had he survived his murder.

TO WEAR A NECKLACE OF SEVEN LEECHES SHOULDN'T BE A PROBLEM AT ALL!

2. A clever slogan that compares my political acumen favorably to various flavored meats.

CUSTERED, THE NEW FLAVOR IN THE POLITICAL MEAT!

3. I thought of a good rhyme but I can't think of the slogan for it. The rhyme is to rhyme my name "Vlumpy Custered" with the phrase "Blusty Pumps". So come up with a kick-tushy slogan that makes that rhyme.

VLUMPY CUSTERED, VITTLETON'S NEW AND REVOLUTIONARY BLUSTER PUMP!!

4. A lot of folks love eggs in Vittleton, but most can't afford the yolk or the white of the egg. They can only afford that little white stringy thing that floats inside the egg that is called the chalaza. Make me a slogan that mentions "chalaza."

DOWN WITH THE CHALAZ-A, WE WANT THE 'YOLK -A'!

5. A slogan to appeal to ladies, something that will make even the most female women in town cream they political jeans. In fact, make sure it includes the phrase "jean cream" in it.

IF THE JEANS ARE VITTLETON THE CREAM YOU NEED IS CUSTERED!

ASSIGNMENT 50 : SEQUELS 102

Dear Answer Masters,

I'm taking a class in how to write sequels. Its actually my second time taking the class, but as they say — "third time's the charmyest".

My assignment is for you to _write a sequel to the "Lullaby Song (Rock-A-Bye-Baby-In-The-Tree-Top)"_ where the baby who fell out of the tree grows up and brutally slaughters everyone who was involved with his "accident". The whole tree falling mishap has left the baby horribly disfigured, but the deepest and most lasting scar is the one... on his soul! Bah hah hah hahhhhh!! (Sorry, I drank to much cinnamon water this morning.)

Now, I know this sequel sounds like it might be scary for the children of this world, but fret not (you simpering little chump), daddy's got a plan: I want that you should set the sequel the _one place_ where kids feel most comfortable... That's right — I'm asking you to set "The Sequel To The Lullaby Song"... (drum roll...) On Top Of Ol' Smokey!

Vance Chumsmun

Sequels 102a
ROCK-A-BYE-BABY SEQUEL

Rock a bye baby, on the treetop,
When the wind blows, the cradle will rock,
When the bough breaks, the cradle will fall,
And down will come baby, cradle and all.

Bahh Ha ha haa now baby back,
Let me know who were there,
Now, Baby wants revenge for there,
Rock a bye baby, on the treetop.

Bahh Ha ha haa are you all ready,
Baby wants slaughter those who were there,
Let me know who were there,
Are you all ready for deaths that were there?

Ha ha haa Baby wants to revenge,
Revenge for the rock of cradle,
Why you there let me rock,
Are you all ready for deaths that were there?

RE: Sequels 102

Dear (mon)S(t)ir,

You just made me your enemy, my friend.

I read your sequel aloud to the children of this town. It has chilled them to their collective bone. A flurry of goose bumps was raised on their terrified skins, and when I tried to calm them with my soothing caress, I discovered that the goose bumps on their flesh happened to spell out a message in Braille. This is that message:

"Daddy, why did the bad essay company ignite this ghastly fear in me?"

Also I think I felt some Braille cuss words. Not cool, guys.

Mercifully, many of the kids have shivered and quivered with such fright and furious intensity that all of their skin has sloughed clean off. Sure, they now have to slather their exposed meatflesh hourly with slick protective salves of all sort, but at least those wretchedly lewd and goosey bumps have seen fit to find solace in other locales, and flown symbolically south for the winter of their discontent.

This is a first rate disaster. The children haven't slept in days. My life is in tatters, my tatters are shattered, and my wife no longer finds me sexually appealing. Here is why:

You have neglected to provide the <u>setting</u> for the rhyme. It was, as you surely remember, supposed to take place "On Top Of Ol' Smokey". Please rewrite the song, this time making it quite clear that the action takes place in that magical land of innocent wonder, far away from where it could threaten any poor, sweet young'uns — ON TOP OF OL' F***ING SMOKEY!!

Vance Chumsmun

Sequels 102a
ROCK-A-BYE-BABY SEQUEL REVISED

Form the rock tree baby fall down,
All were there no one help,
baby lost his family and lover,
For no helping him.

Ha ha ba bathere is pleasure,
But baby will kill,
And a false-hearted lover,
Is worse than a thief.

A baby is killed by those,
Who take what ypu have,
There were all false-hearted lover,
All will slougther by baby now.

The dead baby will decay those,
Those who were there,
Not one baby in a hundred
Now baby can not trust.

All they were hug baby and kiss baby,
And tell baby more lies,
Than crossties on a tree rock,
Or stars in the sky.

RE:RE: Sequels 102

Hey guys,

You win. I give up. Everyone I ever loved has left me in disgust. By the time you read this, I will be stretched out luxuriously on my back in the afterlife, still fuming with fury at the needless torment you have laid at the foot of my head. I guess the *Top Of Ol' Smokey* was too much to ask, huh? And I guess some people (hint: me) just weren't meant to continue slogging through this sick misery commonly called "human existence".

That's right — I'm throwing in the towel on my life. If I had my druthers, I would first wad the towel into a rock-hard ball and throw it right at all your stupid scrotums. But I never get my druthers. I wouldn't know my druthers if they limped right up and bit me on my tushy. And yet, those are my booty biting druthers nonetheless.

So this is my goodbye to the sad old world. I don't want you guys to feel guilty. But you should. Because this is all your fault. If there is another life (and just so you know: *there isn't*) you might get a chance to make it up to me there. Til then, I'll be on top of the Ol' Smokey in the great sky of hell.... watching your every move... staring greedily up the skirt of your soul.

The poignant tragedy of this situation is most elegantly captured with the sublime final words of a magnificent poem I recently read somewhere:

Are you all ready for deaths that were there?

Thank you,

Lexie Kahanovitz for utterly invaluable organizationage & assistance.
David OReilly for impossibly utter visual ninjing.
Justin Heimberg and all the bookies at Seven Footer.
Peter McGuigan and Foundry Literary + Media.
PFFR, UTA, LCK, USA.
The Cheaters Of The World for leading The Way.
All For: Emily and Zadie.

*Names of all companies have been changed to protect the guilty.

About The Author

Vernon Chatman is a three-time Emmy award winning writer/producer on *South Park*, *Louie*, *The Chris Rock Show*, *Late Night With Conan O'Brien*, *China, IL*, and *Delocated*. He is the co-creator/writer/director of the MTV cult hit *Wonder Showzen*, and the [adult swim] cult shits *Xavier: Renegade Angel*, and *The Heart, She Holler*. He also made a thing called *Final Flesh*, for which he apologizes most of all.

About The Illustrator

David OReilly is a person who has a face. He is known for some stuff he did and some other stuff. He lives in a place.